ONE LINE AT A TIME

Why drawing is good for you and how to do it

Claudia Myatt

Dedicated to my father, John Myatt, who always drew,

just for fun, and encouraged me to do the same.

Published in 2020 by Golden Duck (UK) Ltd.

Sokens, Green Street, Pleshey, near Chelmsford,

Essex, CM3 1HT

www.golden-duck.co.uk

Illustrations by Claudia Myatt

Design by Bertie Wheen

Printed by Biddles Ltd.

ISBN 9781899262427

How to Use This Book

You can, of course, start at the beginning and work through. Each chapter deals with a different aspect of drawing, building up your skills and introducing new techniques. Most of the technical stuff is in the early chapters – proportions, perspective, tone and so on. Later, I look at different styles of drawing, trying out new materials, ways to keep you inspired when you feel you're not getting anywhere.

Or you can start where you like, dip in and out, find what you need. The last chapter is a good place to start if you've tried some drawing and given up, as I find ways to change your attitude to 'failure'. Wherever you start, enjoy yourself and keep going. There's no escape. Once you start drawing, you'll never look at life in quite the same way again.

Claudia Myatt

Woodbridge, July 2020

CONTENTS

INTRODUCTION: DRAWING IS FOR EVERYONE   8
The language of line
Why do we find drawing so difficult?

CHAPTER ONE: A DIFFERENT WAY OF SEEING   13
Where do you start?
Draw real things
Trust your eyes not your brain
Switch off your 3D vision

CHAPTER TWO: SHAPES MATTER   20
Measured drawing
Using a viewfinder
The power of negative shapes

CHAPTER THREE: PERSPECTIVE – JUST A POINT OF VIEW   28
Searching for the horizon
The trickery of distance
Changing viewpoints, changing shapes

CHAPTER FOUR: SHADES OF GREY   38
Drawing light and dark
Tonal problems
How to create smooth tones and highlights
Different styles of tonal work
Give yourself time
More about pencils and other drawing tools

CHAPTER FIVE: FIGURES AND FACES   50
Start small, start simple
A quick look at proportions
Figures on the move
What about foreshortening?
Faces and heads
Slow and careful or fast and sketchy?
Life drawing
Hands and feet

Negative shapes again
Figures in perspective

CHAPTER SIX: BEYOND PENCILS   66
                       Sketchbooks and paper
                       Sketching pens
                       Drawing with colour
                       Watercolours
                       Coloured pencils

CHAPTER SEVEN: DIFFERENT WAYS OF DRAWING   80
                       Drawing in public
                       Drawing from photos
                       Drawing a theme
                       Drawing from imagination
                       Drawing words and poetry
                       Journeys, maps and stories

CHAPTER EIGHT: CELEBRATE YOUR MISTAKES   88
                       Upgrade your inner critic
                       Be curious
                       Draw like you mean it
                       We all have 'bad pencil days'
                       Slow down and pay attention
                       There's no such word as 'should'
                       Drawing makes you happy

THE SPIRIT OF DISCOVERY   95

ACKNOWLEDGEMENTS   97

'I think undoubtedly everyone ought to be taught to draw, just as much as everybody ought to be taught to read and write.'

(William Morris)

'Drawing can make us see the familiar as we have never seen it before. It can make us think about seeing, as well as simply seeing.'

(Andrew Marr)

'Drawing is a means of obtaining and communicating knowledge.'

(John Ruskin)

Introduction: Drawing is for Everyone

To sit with sketchbook in hand and try to capture a scene in a few marks of the pencil is a pleasure that runs deep. It enables you to slow down, connect and appreciate what you are seeing because to draw you have to look at something as if you have never seen it before. Drawing, like other absorbing skills – music, dance, ice skating, mountain climbing – takes up our complete attention. Like learning an instrument it takes a while to become fluent, but that's true of anything worth doing.

But there seems to be a perception that drawing is only for the talented – you either tumble out of the womb with a pencil in your hand or you don't, and if you don't then there is no hope for you.

The good news is that this is not true. Drawing is for everyone, not just for those who consider themselves artists, and it's a skill that can be learned.

A few people seem to have a natural gift for drawing, but I think this is rare. My father sketched continuously and as a child, I was fascinated. He was a meteorologist in the days before computers, so his sketchpad was made from the day's spare weather charts which he cut into pocket-sized pieces held together with a bulldog clip. My mother loved parties so we always had a house full of people but as my father was hard of hearing and not able to join in the chatter, he sat at the edge of the room drawing people.

I don't recall that anyone ever paid much attention to what he was doing, quietly in the corner. Drawing was his escape. 'How do you do it?' I asked him. 'Do a little every day', was his reply. I didn't of course, though I try to now.

An early sketch - cautiously discovering the pleasure of telling a story with a few marks

When, later in life, I wanted to draw I had to find out how, one line at a time, one sketchbook at a time. I read books about drawing, I watched artists at work, asked questions. I got together with friends round the kitchen table and practised, I went to life-drawing sessions.

Gradually I started to understand the special way of seeing that you need in order to be able to draw a three-dimensional object onto a two-dimensional piece of paper. This book contains all the practical tips and techniques I learned on the way to becoming a compulsive sketcher and professional illustrator.

The language of line

line   lines   face?   face!

There are of course no lines around things in real life, only an edge where one object ends and another begins. But we use lines as part of the visual language that we are familiar with, as they allow us to recognise and 'read' a drawing. Our brains are so good at this that we find meaning in the simplest of visual shorthand if the lines are at all recognisable. We only need a few familiar clues:

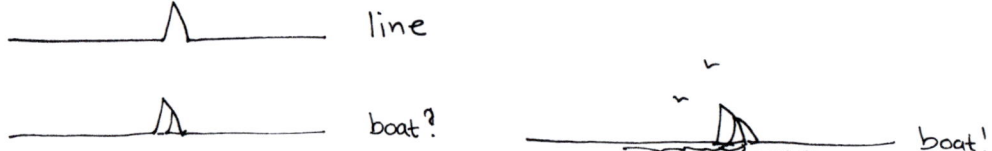

line

boat?

boat!

Images surround us, reminding us that words only go so far and there are times when only a picture will do, from a builder scribbling a diagram on the back of an envelope to symbols and maps and the stories contained within a single photograph or painting.

Drawing can amuse and inform...

Drawing is a language with no need for translation... (this really is a road sign on the Galapagos Islands)

Drawing helps us to learn, remember and appreciate...

Words and pictures go together. We like to know the name of something that interests us. ('What kind of bird is that?') Trying to draw it will add to that understanding and appreciation – and it was the way learning was done in the centuries before cameras.

Why do we find drawing so difficult?

It's mainly because we've never been taught how. As children we draw, naturally, wholeheartedly and without any fear of censure. Then, somewhere around the age of twelve, we usually stop. Education and communication from then on is all about words rather than pictures; we write but, with a few exceptions, we no longer draw. Unless we show a particular flair for art, it is dropped in favour of other subjects. As our verbal skills increase, our visual skills shrink .

I think that we judge our artistic endeavours so harshly because our ability to recognise and understand visual language is far ahead of our ability to do it. As children, we are deluged by images and learn to 'read' picture books at an early age. When it comes to learning written language, our reading and writing skills develop together, but because drawing is never taught in the same way as writing, our visual skills are the equivalent of being able to read *War and Peace* but not even able to write our names. I think this knowledge gap makes us very sensitive to and critical of our delayed learning process.

When, perhaps later in life, we turn once again to drawing and want to appreciate the world around us by keeping a sketchbook, we can't do it. Our fingers, so skilled at handling a pen or tapping a keyboard, turn clumsy and our attempts to draw look like a ten-year-old's.

This appals us so much that the sketchbook goes back in the cupboard, but it's time to start again. Blame your education, not your hands. All we need to do is a bit of catching up.

Go to an art shop or good stationery shop and choose a sketchbook you like the feel of. Choose whatever size feels comfortable.

Most sketchbooks contain smooth white cartridge paper, which is perfect for pencil and pen drawing. Pencils come with hard or soft leads - H for hard, B for soft. There's more about different types of pencils later, but for most sketching B or 2B is best.

CHAPTER ONE: A DIFFERENT WAY OF SEEING

'The whole technical power of painting depends on our recovery of what may be called the 'innocence of the eye'; that is to say, a sort of childish perception of these flat stains of colour, without consciousness of what they signify – as a blind man would see them if suddenly gifted with sight.'

(Ruskin, 'The Elements of Drawing')

A friend of mind once asked her art tutor the secret of his success, how he was able to draw so accurately and elegantly with a few strokes of the pencil. His reply was simple: 'Miles on paper'.

Drawing is like any other skill – the more you do it, the better you get. We learn through repetition. It's how we learn a language, train for a marathon, drive a car, bake a cake. Strangely, art is considered different to other skills, something you either can or can't do, but it really isn't. It's exactly like learning a musical instrument. You need information and then you need practice; loads and loads of practice. It sounds like a hard journey and in some ways it is, but it also extremely rewarding.

The first stages of learning any new skill are hardest because we don't like failure. We like to be able to do things straight away, but with a few rare exceptions that's not how life works. So hold back your inner critic while you wobble your way through a few sketchbooks and put in those miles on paper.

waiting for the ferry to Barra

cloudy & drizzle

Where do you start?

Draw from life wherever possible. It's tempting to copy from photos all the time as drawing real things seems more difficult, but drawing 'real' is the only way to make progress and develop your artist's eye. There's more on how to use photos effectively in Chapter 7.

Draw real things

Start at home. Draw your feet, your partner, your mug of coffee, your lunch, your garden. When you're waiting for something, get out a little sketchbook and draw. Don't wait for a beautiful scene; don't spend all day on holiday looking for the perfect view. Everything becomes interesting when you treat it as a series of shapes and tones.

Once you start drawing anything and everything rather than waiting until you are sitting in front of a pretty scene, your skills will improve rapidly.

You will start to look at everything as potential material, a fascinating arrangement of interconnected shapes.

Now before we learn any new techniques, let's start from where you are. Pick up your sketchbook and a pencil and draw for fifteen minutes. If you're at home, draw whatever is in front of you - a mug of tea, chair, corner of the room, the cat, your feet... anything.

Expect the results to be wobbly and inaccurate because you're at the beginning of the journey and you haven't learnt how to draw yet. Write the date, and make a note on the page of what you found interesting and enjoyable about the process, and also what you found frustrating or particularly difficult.

It's tempting to use an eraser but try not to - leave the wrong lines in and keep going on top. If you keep rubbing out you end up with a hole in the paper!

Start from where you are...

Trust your eyes, not your brain

When we first start trying to draw what we see, the results are usually disappointing, almost embarrassing. We can see the shape we're trying to follow but our drawing of it looks nothing like! Why is it so hard? A pencil is not a difficult tool to use – the way we hold a pen is no different and we have no trouble writing.

The problem is not with our eyes or hand, but with the brain which interferes with how we see. It makes all kinds of decisions on our behalf about perspective, proportion and distance so that we can move around the world safely. It matches what we see with what we know to make sense of everything.

To be able to draw, we need to step aside from the busy, analytical brain and see the world as our eyes see it. To draw an object, we have to look at it afresh, as if we have never seen it before (Ruskin's 'innocence of the eye'). We have to study the shape in front of us as it is from where we are standing, not as we know or remember it, and this takes intense concentration. Here's an example:

What does a flower look like? From your memory it probably looks something like this:

But from where you are standing it is likely to be a different shape entirely. Its outline could be something like the shape below – not particularly flower-shaped at all...

...and it's only the shapes within the shape that enable you to 'read' what it is:

When you change your viewpoint, the object you are seeing changes shape. You know from experience that it's still a flower, but that's no help when you come to draw it and what you see doesn't match the stock image of a flower in your head. You have to look afresh and ask yourself: 'what am I seeing?' For the first time, you have to look with your eyes and forget what your brain knows.

Our heads are full of remembered images and references which cause us to 'look' inwards rather than outwards. We use the phrase 'I see' to mean 'I understand'. This is not a problem until we want to switch off this mental filter that supplies lots of information about the object we are looking at.

It's not easy to focus on a familiar object as if you've never seen it before. The brain will try and interfere: 'You don't need to look at that, it's a flower. I already know what one of those looks like. Here are lots of images already on file to help you identify it from every angle....'

The remembered images in your head will clash with the shapes in front of you and your drawing will be an uneasy mix of the two that leaves you thoroughly dissatisfied.

When a sketch goes wrong, it is partly because you've not spent enough time looking carefully at the subject. We are used to only needing to give something a glance, long enough to recognise it. It's the difference between LOOKING and SEEING. Looking is as different from seeing as listening is from hearing – it's a positive, concentrated action.

When you start to draw, you spend a great deal of time looking at and correcting what's on the page. Of course you need to check what you are putting onto paper, flick your eye between page and scene to make sure there is a match between what you are drawing and what you are seeing, but the focus should be on that intense link between hand and eye which completely bypasses the censor inside your head. You are training your visual memory to hang onto an image in that second between looking at the object and looking at the page.

Try this: draw an object – your hand, a mug, a bunch of keys, a shoe – without looking at the paper at all. Just move your eye slowly around every line and edge of the object and move your pencil at the same speed as your eye.

Don't be tempted to look at the page every time you need to lift and reposition the pencil! The result will be a mess but the process, however frustrating, will take you much closer to the way of thinking you need to draw what you see.

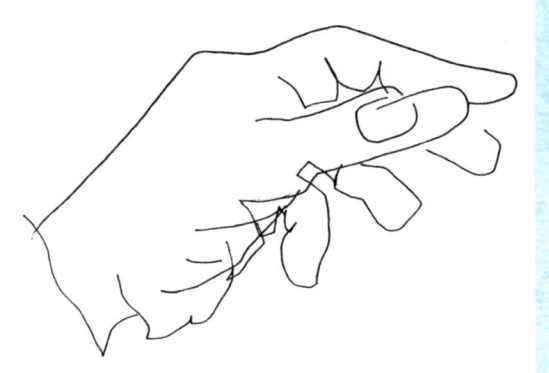

The first drawing was done without looking at the page at all, just linking hand and eye with no attempt to reposition the pencil accurately. The second was done in the same way, but glancing at the paper every time I needed to lift the pencil and place it down again for crossover lines. Try it – it's very good for making you start to look intensely rather than making assumptions about what you are drawing. (There is more about this technique, called 'blind contour drawing' in a book by Betty Edwards called Drawing on the Right Side of the Brain - *a bit of a classic and well worth getting)*

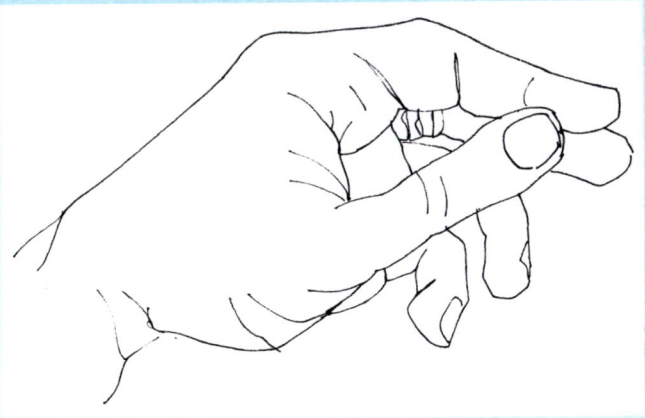

Switch off your 3D vision

You've already started to experience how the brain is an interfering nuisance when it comes to drawing. Not only does it make assumptions about what you see, it makes you wear 3D glasses, so that when your eyes take in the image of a person with a tree coming out his shoulder, experience tells you that in fact they are actually standing at some distance from it.

This is very useful when you want to make sense of the world, but to translate what you see onto a two-dimensional piece of paper, you need to enter a two-dimensional world. It's wonderfully bonkers; it's a flat world with no perspective, where trees emerge from someone's shoulder and a large person at distance is tiny compared to a small person close by.

This is the key to seeing with an artist's eye. When you see everything as flat shapes with no perspective, no overlaps, no depth; when you can draw exactly what is there in front of you, the brain of the person looking at your drawing will be able to convert that information back into 3D in the theatre of their mind. If the information on the page is wrong, it can't do this.

So how do you take off your 3D glasses? Imagine there is a flat sheet of glass between you and what you want to draw. Now think of your piece of paper as being exactly like this window on which you can draw exactly what you see, as you see it, as if your lines were going straight onto the glass. Classical artists called this sheet of invisible glass 'the picture plane', and it will always be right there in front of you, parallel to your eyes.

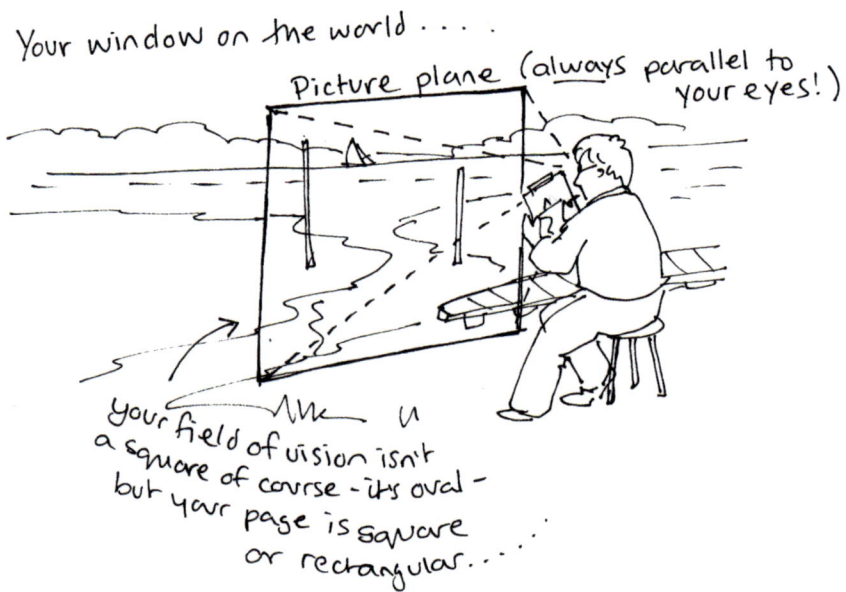

'Parallel to your eyes' means the picture plane is straight in front of you, in the same way that your glasses are parallel to your eyes (unless you've trodden on them and they're on squiffy!). It's like standing in front of the window and looking out, rather than to one side of it. It's a concept that takes five seconds to show in the real world and a page to describe and draw in the two-dimensional world!

You can buy or make from card a rectangular 'viewfinder' to replicate the picture plane and select a scene. There will be more about this in the next chapter, but in the meantime here's an exercise using a readily available picture plane.

Find a window with an interesting (not necessarily beautiful) view. The more complex the view, the better – overlapping roofs and buildings at odd angles are more useful than blobs of foliage.

Firstly, draw the outline of the window shape onto the paper and then draw everything you see, using the rectangle of the window as your frame and reference. It can help to talk through the process as you draw:

'This line starts about halfway up and stops here, then this one comes across at a shallow angle and dips down to the corner; this one starts near the top and meets the other line here....'

This technique helps you to focus purely on the shapes and angles of what you are seeing. It helps if you don't name what you're seeing. This sounds odd, but once you name something your helpful brain will jump in and say 'Aha! I know what that is! This is what it looks like from all different viewpoints...'

But you are drawing only what you can see, from where you are sitting, and nothing else. If you can't see it, don't draw it (even if you know it's there!). Don't peer round corners. If it's an odd angle, then that's what you draw. There will be more about this way of thinking and looking in the next chapters, as it's the key to developing your artist's 'eye'.

Now have another go at the object or scene you sketched at the beginning of this chapter. Imagine that you're drawing onto that window in front of your eyes and see if helps you to begin to see everything as a series of flat shapes and relationships of line.

Draw what you see ... even if it contradicts what you know.

Chapter Two: Shapes Matter

'True boldness and power are only to be gained by care. Even in fencing and dancing, all ultimate ease depends on early precision in the commencement; much more in singing and drawing.'

(Ruskin, 'The Elements of Drawing')

One of the hardest things about drawing is getting shapes and proportions right. To begin with, your drawings look squashed, elongated, distorted, too big in places and too small in others. It can be demoralising but take heart, it's a technical problem with a practical solution.

Drawing is very much about comparison and measuring, and this needs a different way of looking. Habitual, three-dimensional observations such as 'What is it?' 'Who is it?' 'How far away is it?' are of no use to you when trying to draw. You are trying to interpret what you see in front of you as a series of flat lines and shapes, so you have to ask a new set of questions – two-dimensional questions:

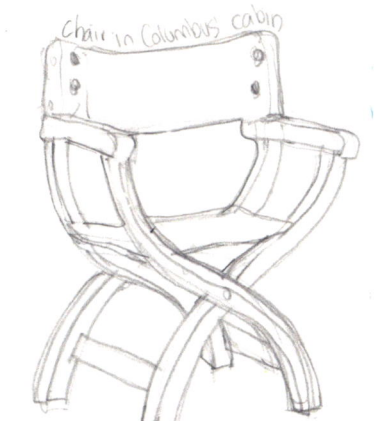

Chair in Columbus' cabin

'How high is that in relation to its width?'

'What shape is that?'

'How long is this line in relation to that one?'

'Where does this line meet that one?'

'What direction does that line go?'

If it helps, ask these questions out loud. You've nothing to lose – everyone thinks artists are eccentric and will make allowances. But some comparisons are not easy to make: for example, can you tell at a glance which of these two lines is longer?

The most important proportions in any drawing are height and width – part of the essential nature of anything is its overall shape. But it's a hard one to judge by eye, so we end up with a dumpy bottle or mug, or boat that's too tall and a beach hut that's too fat.

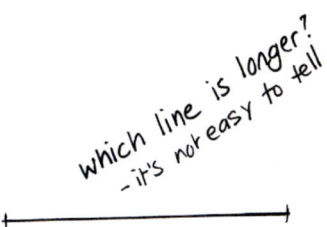

which line is longer? – it's not easy to tell

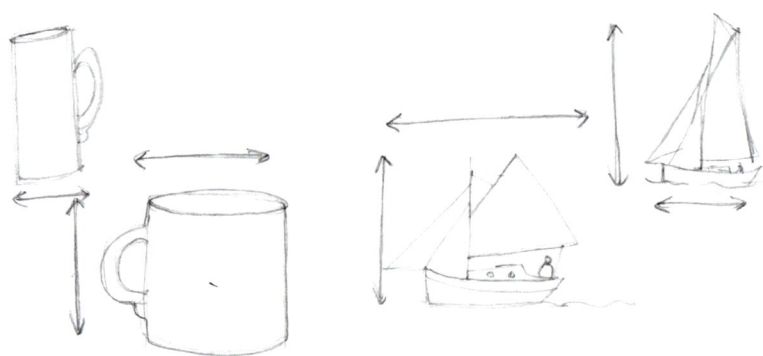

How wide is it compared to how high? If you get that right, you're well on the way.

Measured drawing

Measured drawing is the technique we use to get proportions right, and it goes like this:

Put a mug on a table. Now extend your arm in front of you, shut one eye and use your pencil and thumb as a measuring tool. Starting with the shortest edge (usually the width), use your thumbnail to mark the width as you see it on the pencil.

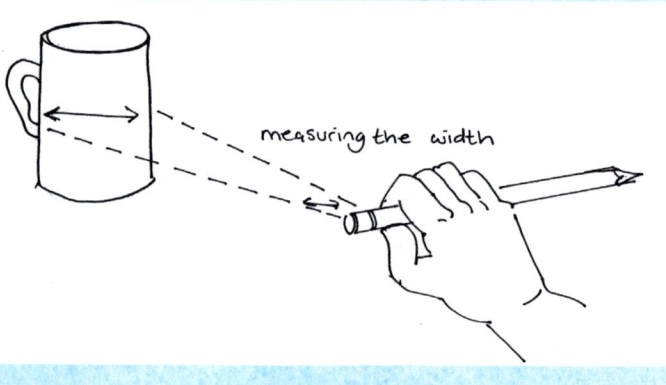

Keep your thumbnail marking the spot and turn your pencil to see how the width compares with the height. Is it the same? Twice as high? In this case it's about three quarters. Yours might be different. Don't get too mathematical, just get close enough.

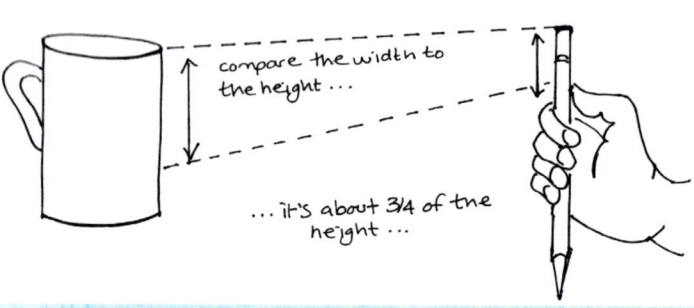

Now transfer these basic proportions to your paper. It's at this stage that it can get confusing, because you might think you have to draw your marks on the page the same size as the measured end of your pencil. Don't! Simply draw your first line – height or width – to whatever size you like. As long as the second line has the same relationship to the first as it did in your pencil measuring exercise, it will look right.. Do your drawing at whatever size fits the page comfortably. All you are doing is comparing one measurement with another.

This process takes a while to describe, so it may sound complicated, but it truly isn't. Once you've got the hang of it, it will be a quick and easy check to make at any stage of a drawing. When you're happy that you've got that basic relationship right – height and width, then you're free to fill in the rest of the drawing, add all the detail, enjoy yourself.

Measured drawing takes the guesswork out of proportions. The more practised you become, the more you train your eye to get these comparisons and proportions right without having to wave your pencil around, but even very experienced artists use this technique.

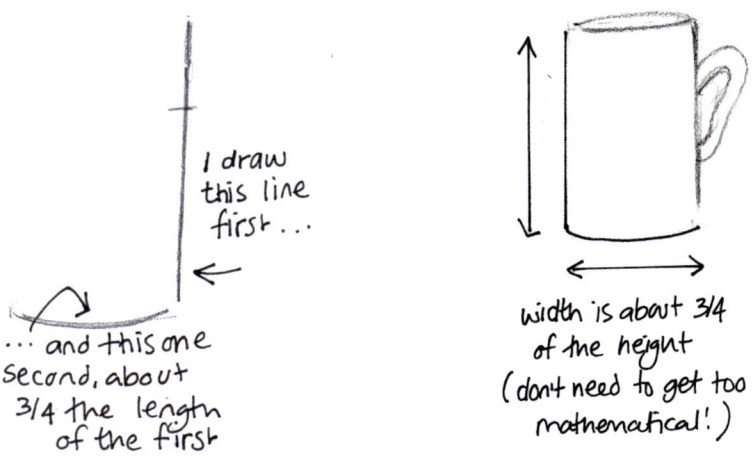

I draw this line first...

... and this one second, about 3/4 the length of the first

width is about 3/4 of the height (don't need to get too mathematical!)

Find a door, cupboard or any other rectangular object. Measure the width and then see how many times that goes into the height. Transfer this relationship to your drawing.

Flick your eyes between the shape on the page and the shape in front of you to see if you've got it right. If you have, then when you fill in the detail it will fit the space much more easily than if you'd just used guesswork.

Keep your arm extended as you measure (if you can). If your elbow is bent for one measurement but not the other, your results won't be accurate. Don't worry about looking conspicuous!

Using a viewfinder

I think another reason why we often get proportions wrong, ending up with dumpy objects and squashed-up landscapes is because of the way our bodies are designed. We move our heads side to side to side to observe a scene; we seldom move them up or down. So we see a wide panoramic scene like this....

But of course our sketchbook page is a rectangle. To squeeze our view onto a page we tend to compress it, which then distorts all the shapes.

It's recognisable of course, but you'll have a frustrating time trying to get the proportions and scale of each object right.

One way to avoid crunching up and distorting the scene is to work to a panorama format. I often go across the spread of a sketchbook page like this.

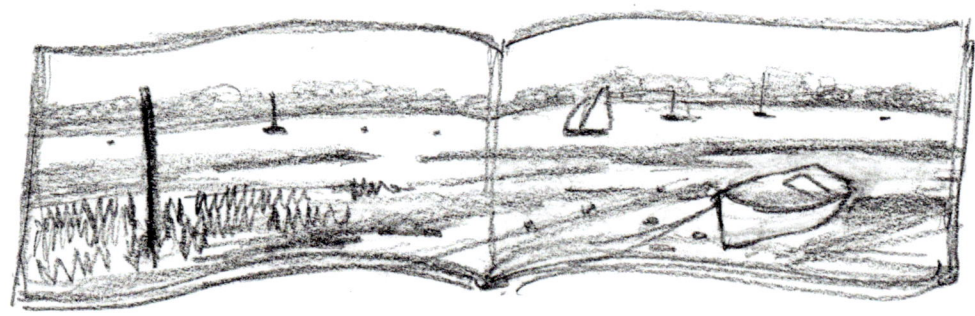

Another useful solution is to borrow a camera's eye and use a viewfinder.

You can buy viewfinders from art suppliers, but it's easy to make your own by cutting a rectangle out of a piece of card or stiff paper, with an aperture about 6 x 4 inches, to make a frame like this:

Go outside with your sketchbook to a place where there is a reasonably open view. Firstly, do a very simple outline sketch of what you can see, without the viewfinder. Don't add any detail, just draw in the basic shapes of trees, hills, fields.

Now look at the scene through the viewfinder (it can help to shut one eye).

Vary the distance you hold it at to zoom in and out, and move it around to find the most pleasing arrangement of shapes. When you've chosen your scene, have another go at a quick sketch using the edges of the viewfinder as the shape of your page.

You may find at this point you need three hands – one to hold the page, another to hold the pencil and another the viewfinder! But once you have the basic reference points in place, noticing where your horizon comes into the side of your rectangle, where that tree or that post is positioned, for example, you can put it down and just use it occasionally to check you're not cramming too much into the scene.

When you compare your two sketches, you may be surprised at just how little a slice of landscape you can fit into a small rectangle. Using a viewfinder can help you to frame and select a scene as well as eliminating the distortion that occurs when you try and pack too much into your drawing.

Using a viewfinder can help you to switch off your 3D vision and see everything as a series of connected shapes – just as we did with the exercise of drawing through a window in Chapter One. This ability to 'flatten' a scene and treat it as if it was two-dimensional is particularly hard to do when you have several miles of scenery in front of you. On location, you might not notice, for example, that the post on the left hand side crosses the line of trees in the distance, or that the sail of the boat goes to the top of the line of trees, or that the river is not the broad expanse you know it to be, but a narrow slice only a bit larger than the distant trees. But if I reduce the scene to a series of flat shapes, it should become easier.

Once you develop the skills to 'see' your scene as a series of flat connected shapes (and you will!), it gives you the vocabulary to express several miles of landscape on a flat page. If you get it right, someone else will read your visual language and translate it into a distant river view inside their mind. That's a bit of magic! And even if no-one else sees your sketch, the act of making it will have engaged you with that place so intensely that you'll never forget it.

The power of negative shapes

Your normal everyday way of viewing the world sees 'things' and not the spaces around them – after all, the objects are important, the empty air isn't. But when you look with your artist's eye and switch off your 3D vision, this changes.

All shapes becomes important, even the ones with nothing in them, because they define the object and make it recognisable. They help us to 'read' the drawing in the same way that the spaces between these words enable us to read the sentence. These empty spaces are called 'negative spaces' and they are a great help when drawing.

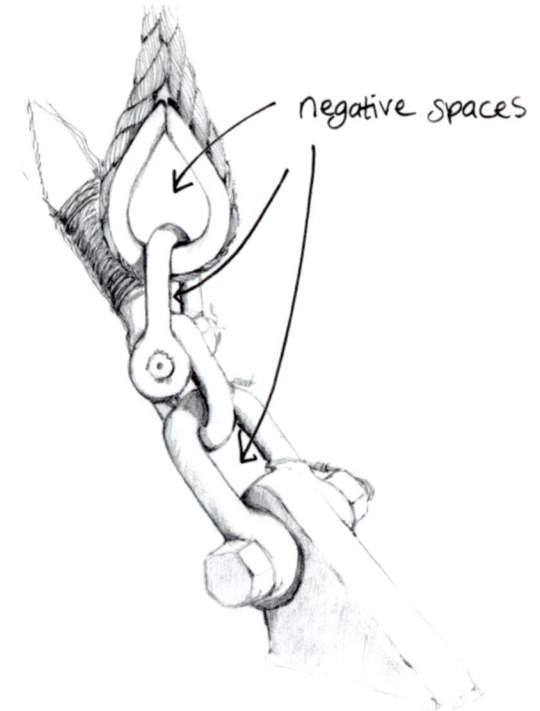

negative spaces

If you can find those spaces and draw them with the same attention to detail as the solid form, they will help you to get everything else in proportion. It can take a while to get your eyes to do this to begin with, as you are used to ignoring empty spaces, but persevere and they will pop into view!

Find a fairly complex object or selection of things to draw as a still life. Good examples would be a vase of lilies, a pot of kitchen utensils, an elaborate chair. Have a go at drawing them in your usual way first, concentrating on the shape of each object.

If you're drawing a chair, position it so that it's at an angle, with plenty of awkward corners and shapes to work out.

Now try again paying particular attention to the negative shapes, all those different-shaped spaces in between. Remember to stop thinking of them as three-dimensional spaces; from your viewpoint they are flat shapes. If it helps, use a small viewfinder zoomed in close to give you plenty of negative spaces around the edges of the object as well as within it.

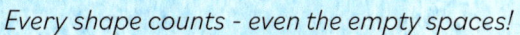

Every shape counts - even the empty spaces!

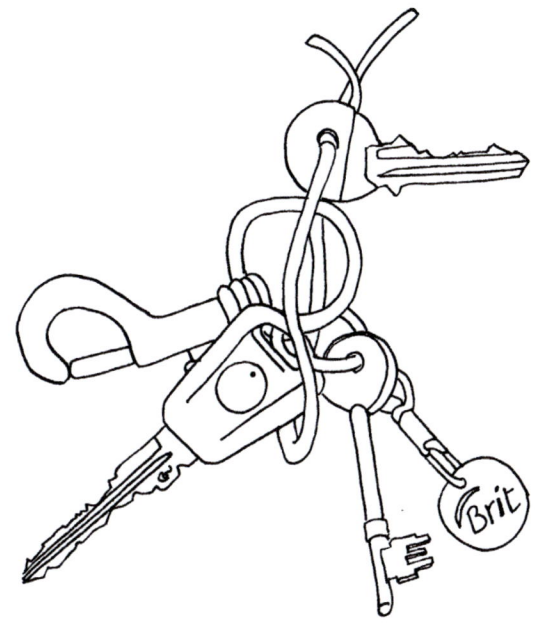

CHAPTER THREE: PERSPECTIVE — JUST A POINT OF VIEW

Perspective: (dictionary definition)

(1) the art of representing three-dimensional objects on a two-dimensional surface so as to give the right impression of their height, width, depth, and position in relation to each other.

(2) a particular attitude towards or way of regarding something; a point of view.

Most artists find perspective a challenge – I certainly did. Drawing something 'in perspective' means you are dealing with odd angles and difficulties of scale, so there is a bigger than usual contradiction between what you know and what you are seeing.

In this first drawing, it's reasonable to assume that the lines represent something upright, like a post. The second drawing confirms this, as we can tell from the context that it is a post, vertical lines to represent a vertical object.

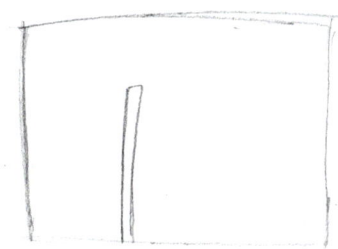

But the next drawing is more ambiguous. It could still be an upright post, one that is tapering, perhaps?

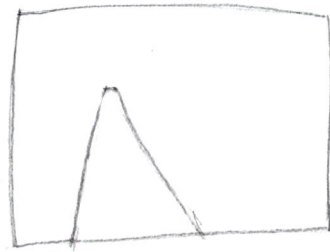

By the time we place it in context, assuming I have drawn the lines correctly, it's impossible to 'read' it as upright any more. It has now become a pontoon – a horizontal object represented by vertical lines. As hard as you try, you cannot see it in any other way, just as if I show you the word 'cat' and try to tell you it's a dog.

So we can 'read' the language of perspective drawing very well indeed. But to 'write' it for ourselves, we need to stop and work out how to get the language right. It's like looking at the individual letters of the words rather than jumping straight to the meaning of the sentence. For the illusion of perspective to work, the angles and relative sizes of each line need to be correct. If they're not, the image is unreadable, like a word misspelt.

If like me you are not mathematically minded, drawing perspective seems to involve a confusing list of rules and formulae. The words 'vanishing points' and 'two point perspective' were enough to make my heart sink. But I found that once I understood the basic principles I could do without the complicated technical understanding. If you are particularly interested in architectural drawing or townscapes you may well need to dig deeper (and there are plenty of good books on the subject), but I'm going to focus on the three things you need to know and some techniques to help your drawings look 'right' without getting too technical.

(1) – Searching for the horizon

Before I started sketching I hadn't realised that the horizon is always at eye level. That's your eye level as the invisible artist – not necessarily the eye level of the people in the sketch unless you're all on level ground and sharing the same eye level (give or take variations in our height).

Next time you go to the coast, make a point of noticing where the horizon is. If you stand on top of the highest cliff, the horizon is at your eye level. When you go and lie down on the beach, the horizon has dropped - it's still at your eye level down there.

In the image on the right, I'm the artist standing...

...but in this, one, I'm the one sitting.

Why do we need to know this?

Firstly, so that we can place things (and people) correctly on the page.

Secondly, the horizon – whether you can see it or not - splits the page. Above it, we see the underneath of an object; below it, we see the top. If you're drawing complicated shapes and get confused about how much of anything you're seeing, it can help to bear this in mind.

Thirdly, because everything we see gets smaller and smaller towards that line until it disappears (more on this later).

If you are placing figures in your drawings, their eye level may or may not be the same as yours...

In the drawing of the couple on the bench, I have the same eye level as the people in my scene. I am obviously sketching on a similar bench behind them!

But in the this scene, my viewpoint is different to the all the figures in the picture. I'm standing on a cliff which is slightly lower than the one on the other side of the bay.

It's useful to know where your eye level is when you start to draw, even when you can't see the horizon. In a street scene, it can be helpful to draw it as a line across the page so that you can keep everything in scale and in the right place on the scene.

eye level

This may seem confusing and/or irrelevant at the moment, in which case file it away for future reference. It will come in useful as your drawing progresses, I promise!

Wherever you are right now, look straight ahead and imagine a line across your eyes, dividing your world in two.

Now pick up a mug and hold it so that the top is at eye level. What shape is the top of the mug? Now lower it a few inches. What shape is the top now? Lower it further, notice how the ellipse grows as you lower it. Only when you are finally looking down on it does it become the shape you know and recognise – round.

Now arrange two or three mugs at different levels in front of you and try and draw them.

above eye level, the underneath becomes visible

on the horizon, you see neither above nor below ..　　　　EYE LEVEL

... the further below eye level you go, the more of the top of an object you'll see

the bottom of the mug will be a little bit more curved than the top as it is further from eye level than the top!

The sides of each one will all be the same - vertical - but the shapes at the top and bottom will vary. If you get confused, remember the picture plane - that window in front of your eyes.

Take off your 3D glasses and focus on the shapes your eyes are seeing as if you were tracing the image from a photograph.

Measured drawing can help here. It's so hard to judge how wide to make that ellipse, as your brain will be telling you 'it's a round thing!' and you try and find a compromise between what you see and what you know. The result pleases neither your eyes nor your brain!

But if you hold your pencil upright and measure the width of the ellipse, you can measure how many times that goes into the height of the mug,. This will help you get the right shape, using the 'language' of perspective.

(2) - The trickery of distance

Yes, of course you know that things appear smaller when they are further away from you, but do you realise how much smaller they get, and how quickly? We know that everything recedes into the horizon, so your brain reads the shapes and position on the page to let you know without even being asked that you are looking at a large object far away rather than a small object close up.

Both objects are drawn a similar size in this sketch – but we know without question that the bird is a small object close up and the boat is a large object further away.

If I switch the objects round, what happens? Both objects are still the same size on paper – but not in your head!

We are used to the convention that nearer objects are at the bottom of the page and further away objects are towards the horizon (or generally, the further objects are higher up the page in a landscape as there is often just sky at the top of the page). Any variation from this order throws our brain into confusion.

Look out of the window at something in the street - a tree, a car, anything. Hold up your hand and see how big the object is between finger and thumb.

Has the car parked in the street or the boat on the river shrunk to a couple of centimetres within the distance of a few metres? Did you realise just how much and how quickly objects shrink with distance?

It's easy to underestimate how much smaller objects look at quite short distances. If you're struggling with trying to get elements of a landscape to fit the scene, check that you have their relative sizes right. Use measured drawing to compare one thing to another.

On a landscape scene you might be looking at a depth of several miles, so it's all too easy to get distant objects too big - and close up objects too small. If in doubt, measure and compare one object with another, with pencil and thumb, or even with a ruler.

(3) - Changing viewpoints, changing shapes

In Chapter One we looked at how the shape of a familiar object varies depending on our viewpoint, but we recognise it from any angle because of our knowledge about it and all the visual clues within what we see.

what your brain sees...

what your eyes see...

You can draw an object from one position, then take two steps to the left, look at it again. Your brain reassures you that it's the same object, but from your eye's viewpoint it has become a different shape and needs to be looked at afresh.

Same object, different shape...

Many words that apply to drawing apply to thinking and reasoning too. A discussion will include the phrases: 'Look at it from my point of view', 'from this perspective...'

So much about seeing happens at an unconscious level, but to draw we need to make those observations conscious.

Measuring angles

When drawing an object 'in perspective' - that is, from any other viewpoint than face on, you have the problem of sloping lines and angles to deal with.

You know when you look at this drawing that lines A and B are parallel to each other, parallel to the ground, and that this is a normal house not a crooked one, even though the lines drawn are sloping. This is because the lines are correct for this viewpoint (or close enough!).

Our brains are used to this apparent contradiction and have made a rapid translation: 'It's a normal house just looked at from a different viewpoint'.

But when you come to draw it, the difference between what you see and what you know causes confusion. You can't please both your brain and your eyes, so you try and compromise, which pleases neither. When the lines and angles you have drawn are badly wrong, we can't do the bit of magic in our heads that makes a two-dimensional set of lines become a three-dimensional object. This one is just a wobbly house!

Getting angles right is key to drawing in perspective. Some are easy to recognise – you can usually tell when something is more or less than 90 degrees, but the more subtle ones can be harder to pin down.

does the line slope up? or down? hard to tell!

you need help to get these subtle angles right.

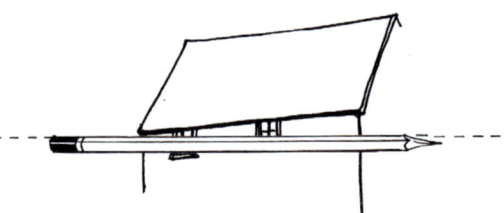

It helps to hold your pencil up horizontally in front of your eyes to see whether a line dips above or below the horizontal and by how much. Hold the pencil level - now you can see exactly how much the roof line slopes up to the right.

That elusive eye level/horizon line can come in useful here, as lines above the horizon will dip towards it and lines below the horizon will rise up to meet it. You'll also notice that the furthest corner of the house is smaller than the nearer one, as it's further away. So all three principles of perspective start to come together and hopefully will help you make sense of what you are seeing.

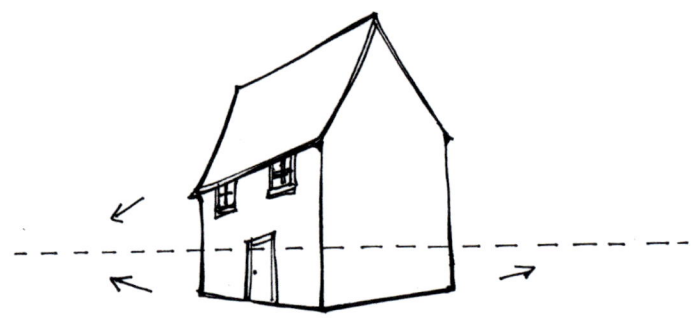

Awareness of where eye level is may help you work out which way lines are going.

A great tool for measuring angles in a drawing is a small folding ruler (available from high street stationers).

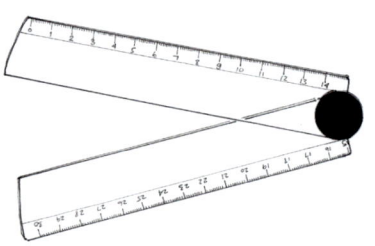

Line one side of the ruler against the vertical or horizontal line, then adjust the other side until it matches what you see. Now transfer this directly to the page for an accurate angle.

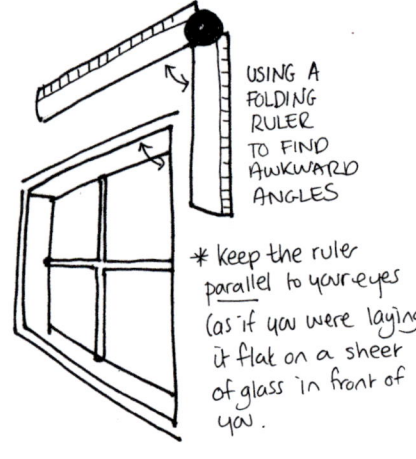

USING A FOLDING RULER TO FIND AWKWARD ANGLES

* keep the ruler parallel to your eyes (as if you were laying it flat on a sheet of glass in front of you.

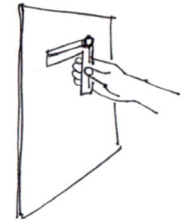

If you don't have a folding ruler, you can make one out of card, or use your finger and thumb for a rough guide.

This is particularly useful for buildings and structural shapes, as you'll find that the angles of an object in perspective dip away much more sharply than you think. Make sure you keep the angle finder parallel to your eyes - flat against the picture plane. It helps to support the evidence of our eyes whenever it is in contradiction to what our brain is telling us that we know.

If you measure and observe what is actually there and transfer that to the page, it will look right. Honestly. You will be drawing 'in perspective' from observation, without the need for construction lines and vanishing points.

Find a corner of a room and draw a simple outline of everything in that corner. You don't need to go into too much detail. Use the folding ruler to get the angles of the ceiling in perspective.

Now move to a different position, from one chair to another, perhaps. Look at the scene again – same object, but different angles, shapes and overlaps. It needs studying afresh – only the vertical lines will stay vertical as in the previous sketch.

Finally.....

TRUST YOUR EYES AND NOT YOUR BRAIN

Don't get too bogged down by rules of perspective. The only thing you really need to remember is that your tricky brain is making all kinds of decisions and assumptions on your behalf about what you are seeing. If in doubt, deal with what is actually in front of you, right now, from where you are standing. Forget what you know, look hard at what you are seeing.

If you move to a different position, your brain will tell you that you are looking at the same object, but you won't be – it will be a different shape. It all depends on your 'point of view'!

pink amaryllis at June's flat

doodling while chatting to June

24th February

CHAPTER FOUR: SHADES OF GREY

'Take care that shadows and lights be united, or lost in each other; without any hard strokes or lines; as smoke loses itself in the air, so are your lights and shadows to pass from the one to the other, without any apparent separation.'

(Leonardo da Vinci)

So far the focus of this book has been about drawing lines and trying to capture shapes. But your instinct when sketching most landscapes and objects, especially subtle scenes like a sunset, will be to shade in areas of light and dark. This is called using tone.

Usually drawing will use a combination of the two techniques, line and tone. Sometimes you may want to use line alone, sometimes tone, sometimes both. Adding tone is a clever piece of artist's trickery. It's how we show the fall of light on an object and give the illusion that you are not looking at a flat piece of paper but a proper three-dimensional object or scene.

Drawing light and dark

Tone is another part of the 'alphabet' of drawing. Here's an example:

There's not enough information in this drawing to recognise what the object is. Could be a pebble, an egg, a pond seen from above…. If it was drawn as part of a scene we could make sense of it, but on its own there's not enough to go on.

If I start to add tone, something happens in your brain and you will now start to see this as a smooth, rounded three-dimensional object. It's not, of course – it's on a flat piece of paper, but the shades of grey are having the same effect on you as the sloping lines in a perspective drawing; it's a recognised language of perception. You can try and see this as a flat shape which is coloured grey on one side, but it's not easy. It will keep popping into 3D!

If I do some more tonal work on this drawing the illusion is complete. Putting the light edge against a dark background and adding a patch of grey for a shadow tells us that we are looking at an egg – on a table, with the light coming from the left. It has become more than a few patches of grey.

If you take a tonal drawing far enough, the lines disappear and there are only areas of different tone, one against another. You'll notice that we don't need colour to 'read' pictures, we only need shapes and tones. Colour is a bonus!

So now you need to get familiar with the language of tone and start to use all these shades of grey that a pencil can do so well.

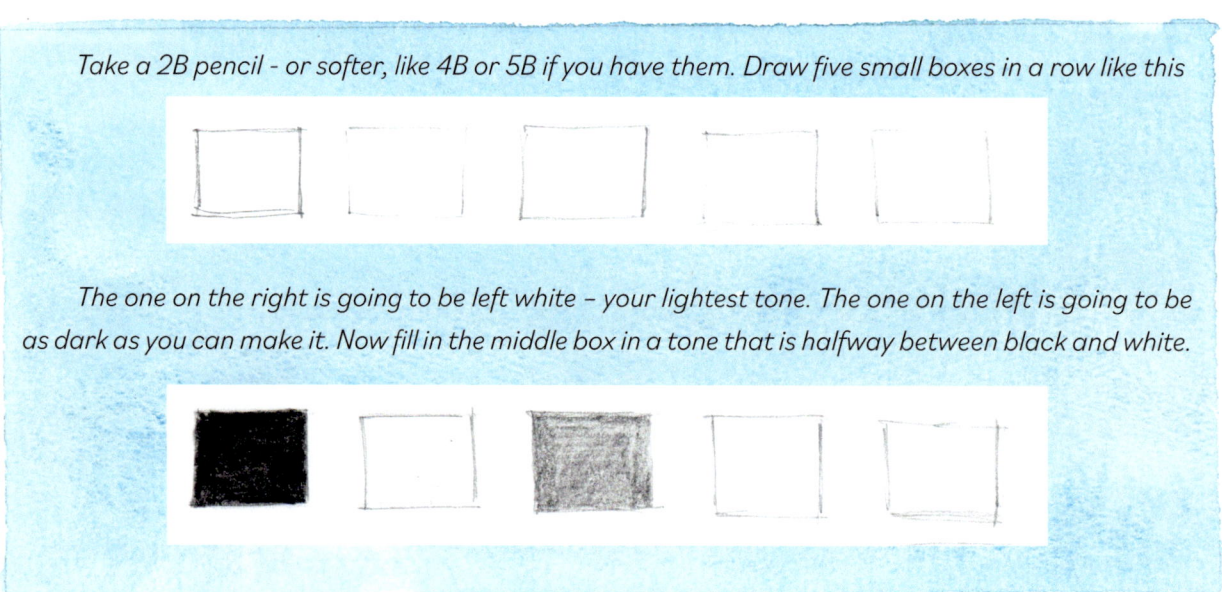

Take a 2B pencil - or softer, like 4B or 5B if you have them. Draw five small boxes in a row like this

The one on the right is going to be left white – your lightest tone. The one on the left is going to be as dark as you can make it. Now fill in the middle box in a tone that is halfway between black and white.

Then do the ones in between, again trying to get them halfway in tone between the ones on either side. You should end of with an equal grading from light to dark like this:

dark ← ——————→ light

You can do this with any number of squares, of course, but five is a manageable place to start. It can take a while to get used to how much pressure to put on the pencil to get the exact shade of grey you want.

When drawing lines, you tend to use the point of the pencil, but when shading tones it's easier to work at a shallow angle so you get broader strokes and can put more pressure on without breaking the point. Softer pencils (3B-9B) will give you blacker tones more quickly, but they'll be a bit messier!

Now try the same thing as a continuous bar of gradual tone from dark to light:

Now try the egg shape, using all the shades of grey that you've just been practising.

If your tonal work is careful enough, the original lines you drew will now have disappeared. You can see that the way to show the lightest area is by adding a contrasting tone next to it.

You may find to begin with that it's not as easy as it looks to get a gently graded tone and a clean edge, but that's only because you haven't done it much before and your hand isn't used to it. Stick with it and it will get easier.

Tonal problems

How's your egg looking? If it looks something like this, don't despair. There are two problems that usually come up when you begin to work with tonal drawing, both of them easily solved with a bit of concentration and practice.

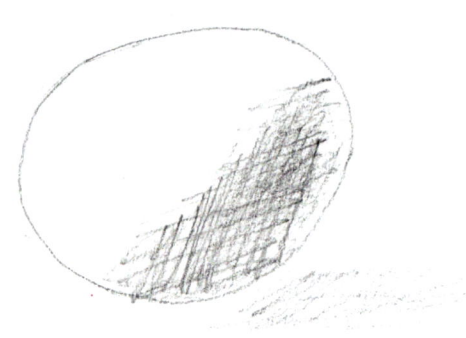

1. Avoid fuzzy edges

When working in tone, pay attention to where one tone ends and another begins or the drawing won't read properly. This usually means just slowing down a bit when you meet another edge.

fuzzy edges make image hard to 'read'.

practice shading to a clean edge with an even tone

rub with your finger to get an even shade

now it looks as though the sky goes behind the boat

In the sketch above it looks as if the sky has skidded to a stop around the edge of the sails, which destroys the illusion that the sky goes behind the boat. Making a clear division between sky and sail will make the illusion complete.

2. Make your shading go with the flow

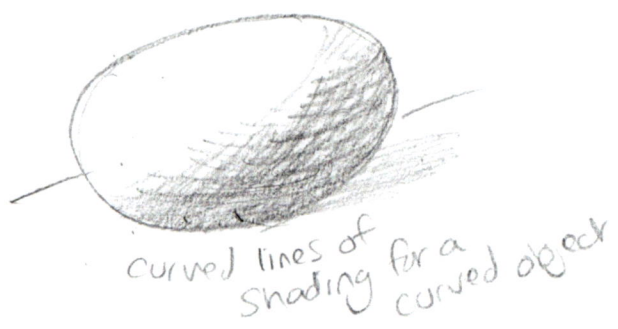

curved lines of shading for a curved object

There are many ways of showing tone. In this drawing, the shading is done with scribbled lines called cross-hatching. This can work well, but straight lines don't help to create the illusion of a round object. If you want to use this technique, make sure the lines fit the subject and use curved lines for a curved surface.

So there are many ways to make tonal marks, from smoothly blended to loose and scribbly. Play around with all the various options and techniques and see what suits you best. There's more about the different types of pencils and tonal tools at the end of this chapter.

How to create smooth tones and highlights

If you like the idea of creating smooth, blended tones with your pencil, there are a number of ways to do it. Try some of these:

1. Smudge with your fingers – effective but a bit messy!

2. Use blending tools like this:

Also called blending stumps or tortillons, they are made out of compressed cardboard and you can buy a set of different sizes. They're more effective (and less messy!) than fingers.

3. Use an eraser to create highlights

You can use an eraser as a drawing tool to create light areas. Shave the corner to a point with a scalpel if you need a fine point. You can also buy a refillable detail eraser, or a fine tipped electric one, to help you draw with some precision.

refillable eraser

4. Work in a variety of different pencils

Experiment and see what works. Use HB for fine lines, going down to 6B or softer for deep shadows. You can also buy water-soluble drawing pencils. I've used a wet brush to create the soft greys on this figurehead drawing.

5. Use a smooth paper

Slightly rough paper, like watercolour paper, will give you a textured tonal area like the spiral sketch on the previous page. Sometimes this is useful – it's your choice. Most sketchbooks contain a reasonably smooth cartridge paper but if you really want to do some very realistic, detailed tonal work, check the paper surface before you begin. I have more to say about different types of paper and sketchbook in Chapter 6.

'To Sea No More' ~ Fishing boats, Camaret

I don't normally have the patience for this kind of detailed tonal drawing (above), but these derelict fishing boats on the beach at Camaret in Brittany must have kept me busy for hours. I can't remember, but I suspect that I started this on location and then finished off all the detail later from a photo. If this is the kind of style you are aiming for, be prepared to spend many enjoyable hours on one drawing (and if your attention wanders, leave it and come back later or you'll get careless and spoil it).

Another thing to remember is that you have the full range of greys to use, from the deepest black to the softest grey. Don't be afraid to get some weight into those dark places when you need them.

It's tempting to shy away from making strong, confident marks when you're a beginner! On this quick coastal sketch there was a strong contrast between the lower part of the cliffs and the white sails. I needed to go in strongly with the dark area or else the sails would have got lost.

Different styles of tonal work

Tonal drawing doesn't have to be done with smoothly blended shades of grey. Pencils are incredibly versatile tools and there is a wide variety of ways to make expressive tonal marks. The important thing is that they should suit both the subject and the style of the drawing, whether it's a carefully considered studio piece or a rapid five minute sketch on location.

This sketch of a boat at low tide was done on location. You can tell that the pencil has moved fast, but there is still enough clarity of line where it's needed. You gradually learn when to move your pencil fast and when to slow down!

Different kinds of scribbled shading are used for different subjects – look at the difference between the marks I've made for the trees, the boat's planking and the foreground mud.

Rocks are a good subject for tonal drawing. Smooth shading wouldn't have been right for these rugged-edged rocks in Pembrokeshire so I used rough cross-hatching for the rocks and a smoother more even shading for the sand. Again, this was a quick sketch done on location.

This sketch of a wildlife photographer was done fast on a moving boat. I focussed on the lines and the only tonal work I had time for was the contrast between the dark camera and the light hand and face. I've tried to be as clear-edged there as I could before the photo was taken and the subject moved.

Give yourself time

Whether you sketch slowly and carefully, or fast and scribbly, it will take time to become fluent. The pencil is such a simple and familiar tool that you will be frustrated to be taking so long to get confident with your drawing. But it takes your hand a while to catch up with what your brain now knows. It's like watching the grace and ease with which an experienced player's hands flow over the piano keyboard when you're still slowly and haltingly learning your first tune. That ease of movement is all down to familiarity, and there are no short cuts so give yourself a chance. Do you remember how long it took to become easy with handwriting? Don't expect too much of yourself too soon. Gradually you will find your own ways of combining line and tone to show the 'solidness' of things that you draw.

Drawing from life makes you go straight to the essentials – in this case the strong, geometric forms of the rock and the clear, dark silhouette of the cormorant. (I clearly wasn't happy with the shape of the cormorant on the rock so I had another go at getting those slightly hunched wings.)

Now it's your turn:

Use a soft pencil – 2B is fine – and experiment with tonal textures.

Play around with all the different ways there are of creating the feeling of solid objects with all their different surfaces, from rough to glossy. Try these: grass, trees, ripples on water, clouds, pebbles, wood, mud, anything else you can think of.

different pencil marks for trees, bushes, fields & hedges ...

A word of warning... shading and playing around with tones can be very enjoyable, as it adds substance and shape to a drawing. BUT make sure your core shapes and proportions are sound first. There's a tendency to try and rescue a hesitant drawing by adding shading, in the hope that will make it all right. It doesn't work!

More about pencils and other drawing tools

2B or not 2B...

Now you've had a go at working with tones as well as lines, this is a good time to experiment with different types of drawing tools. You may already have bought a set of drawing pencils which have the full range from H (hard) to B (the B is for 'black', though we call them soft). Soft pencils are good for shading and strong, expressive lines. Hard pencils like H or HB give you fine clear lines but they don't rub out easily and are no good for shading. Most of the time I use a 2B which is a good all rounder for both lines and shading, or a B if I'm doing more careful line drawings.

Keep it sharp

I know it sounds obvious, but do keep your pencils sharp. A scalpel gives you a far better point than a pencil sharpener, and for very precise work you can get a fine point by rubbing the sides on sandpaper or sharpening stone. If you don't like using a scalpel, then make sure you get a decent quality pencil sharpener.

Other types of pencils

Clutch pencils save you having to keep sharpening, and give you a constant, clear line. You can buy different leads – I have one with a B and another with a 2B. A fine clutch pencil like this is perfect for detailed line drawing...

.... and a big chunky clutch pencil like this (made by Cretacolor) is great for strong shapes and fast, expressive shading.

You can buy a variety of leads for this, soft or hard (I use 2B) and also different colours – sepia and brown as well as grey.

There are many more variations on the humble pencil now than ever before. You can buy graphite sticks - pencils without the wood surround, good for broad tonal marks. There are also now water-soluble pencils which enable you to create soft and subtle greys with a wet brush. Shop around, experiment, see what suits you.

Charcoal and chalky pencils

Charcoal is good for expressive mark making, especially if you like to work large scale, but it can be messy. Conte crayons are chalky pencils that come in a sepia and white as well as black. Some sketching sets will contain a range of pencils, charcoal and conte crayons - try them all!

A note about holding pencils

To begin with, you will probably hold your pencil like you hold a writing pen. After all, that's what your hand is used to. But gradually start to experiment with different ways to hold your pencil or drawing tool. Try a looser, more relaxed grip for smooth, sweeping marks and a closer, tighter hold for fine detail. Try holding the pencil half way up rather than close to the point; try working standing up at an easel with charcoal or a graphite stick, see what suits your way of drawing. Changing your way of holding the pencil, or changing your drawing tool, can sometimes help you loosen up if you find you've become stuck and want to make more confident marks.

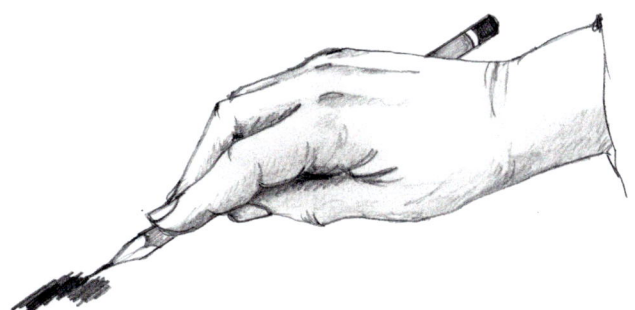

And finally a word about erasers...

The most useful property of pencils is of course that you can rub the marks out, though this can be a mixed blessing. Trying to correct heavy areas of pencil tone can leave you with a smudgy mess. There are several types of erasers, and I prefer fairly hard ones like Staedtler Mars plastic which is soft enough not to damage the paper. I've never got on with putty rubbers; they just seem to smudge everything and disintegrate into a mucky lump.

Birdwatchers on the ferry....
sea eagles, golden eagles
spotted

also puffins, guillemots, razorbill, shags

CHAPTER FIVE: FIGURES AND FACES

Figure drawing can be daunting but at some stage you will want to add people to the scenes you draw. Ruskin was rather snooty on the subject:

'I do not think figures, as chief subjects, can be drawn to any good purpose by an amateur. As accessories in a landscape they are just to be drawn on the same principles as anything else.'

It's true that drawing figures in detail, portraiture and life drawing all require careful study, but adding people to a landscape or doing simple figure sketches need not be too difficult if we do as Ruskin suggests and treat the figure in the same way that we treat every part of the scene, as a series of shapes and related lines.

The prospect of drawing a fellow human can be alarming but I don't think figures are any more difficult to draw than anything else; it's just that if they are wrong, even the tiniest bit wrong, we are so hypersensitive to the human form that we notice immediately. The other difficulty is that people are rarely still, and every slight change of posture or action gives us a completely different shape to deal with.

One of the problems with drawing people is that they are usually on the move, or busy doing something. This means you have to go straight to the heart of what's important, so it's great practice. The lady in the yellow satin skirt and trainers caught my eye in Havana and luckily I was in a cafe with my sketchbook already out so I managed to catch her colours as she walked past.

The guitarist was done quickly too, in a fairly dark room. I had to wait for his hand position to repeat so that I could get the shape of his arms and shoulders. You can see that as long as you capture the essence of the scene, get a few important shapes down, your brain will supply all the missing detail and overlook the raggedy bits!

Start small, start simple

Anything complex is easier drawn at a distance and the same goes for people. From a distance a figure is a blob, a bit like this:

Forget you are looking at a three-dimensional person; what you are seeing is a two-dimensional shape. Try and capture it in a few lines and tones. What will probably come out first is a series of symbols or visual stereotypes while your brain tries to get to grips with what you want to do. Keep going, keep asking the question: 'What am I actually seeing?'

Your first attempts may look more like stick men, and the heads will usually be too big, like the one on the right:

Heads are smaller than we think and legs are longer. At a distance the legs taper, especially if the figure is walking, and you can't see feet in detail. The upper torso seems wider because of the arms and often there are more layers of clothing on the upper body...

Clothes, hairstyles, posture and age all help to create variations in what you see. If you're having trouble with this exercise, find a page in a magazine with plenty of people on it, and trace over the outlines on the page to get a feel for the shapes you'll need to draw.

James Wharram

Once you have the hang of these distant figures, try bringing them closer. Again, forget about any detail and concentrate on the overall form.

Many of my quick sketches are done in pen rather than pencil. I usually have a sketching pen or biro in my bag or pocket; they never need sharpening and you can't rub out, so you just have to go for it. Good for rapid sketching! I'll be looking at pen and other drawing media in more detail in the next chapter.

Draw the back view

Drawing figures in public can be embarrassing because, instinctively, people seem to know when they are being sketched. When you get more experienced you can brazen this out (and be prepared to show them the sketch), or get clever at looking sideways and pretending to be drawing something else, but to begin with I recommend drawing figures with their back to you. This has the added advantage that you don't need to draw the face, which is another set of challenges entirely!

To begin with, don't do the whole figure. Find a cafe or public place where there are seated figures who are likely to stay reasonably still for a while, or if you're worried about drawing in public, you can do this with friends or family at home.

Draw the head and shoulders only, concentrating on the shapes and outline, the detail of the hair and neckline at the back of the shoulders. Add part of the chair if you want to.

Draw only what you can see. If they are wearing glasses but you can only see a corner of the frames and lenses, just draw the little bit of the shape you can see. It takes time, as with any drawing, to exclude what you know and only include what you can actually see, in the shape you are seeing it.

As you build up confidence, include more of the figure – arms and hands on the table holding a cup of coffee or reading a book.

Focus on the folds of the clothes and the shapes that they form. Have a go at three quarters view so you get a bit of the face.

One thing is for sure – you will never run out of subjects and you'll have hours of wonderful figure drawing practice without ever having to 'face' a single portrait!

A quick look at proportions

Most of the time, proportions are hard to judge as people tend to be doing things; sitting, standing or moving. You will rarely draw them standing straight up in front of you with arms down by their side. But it's worth remembering that we have a tendency to make heads too big and legs too short. I think this is because the face is the most important thing we look at when we communicate with each other, and so we 'see' it as bigger.

You will probably remember that when a human is standing straight, the head goes into the body eight times, and it's worth bearing this in mind. This is how it looks (see the figure on the next page):

Elbows are at waist level, and finger tips go down to the mid thigh. The halfway point of the human figure is about the level of the hips (yes, legs are longer than we think)

There are several approaches you can take to drawing figures, but if you struggle to get everything in proportion you might find the following technique useful. I learned it in life drawing classes and found it very helpful for giving my figures a more 'solid' look.

It starts with a stick man - give it a try:

1. Start with a head and spine:

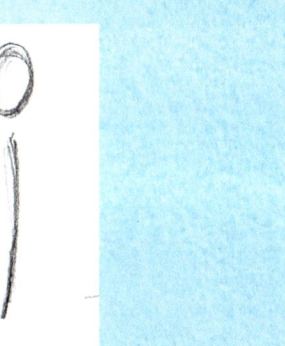

2. Then add a line for the shoulders and hips:

3. Now add the arms and legs:

4. Add wedges of shapes for the hands and feet:

5. Now flesh out the skeleton and add clothes:

6. Rub out the construction lines and add as much detail as you need:

Figures on the move

Get hold of some photos of figures in action – the sports section of a newspaper is good for this. Take a felt pen and draw the stick figure over the photo (or use tracing paper if you don't want to damage the photo). Draw the line of the spine, shoulders and hips, then arms and legs. Next, try drawing your own action figures. I found this technique especially useful for drawing cartoons. You'll notice that if the shoulders tilt one way, the hips will always tilt in the opposite direction:

hips and shoulders balance each other...

More figures on the move

The stick figure exercise should give you a good foundation and help to develop an instinctive feel for what looks right.. But when people move fast you may not have time to plan. Have a go at drawing figures from the TV screen. Look out for patterns and repeat movements to catch a bit more of a line every time the figure repeats a move. Don't rub anything out, just keep the pencil moving. It will train your powers of observation even if the results are nothing but fragments and mad scribbles!

Once you feel more confident, try drawing when you're out at a sporting event, concert or dance. Use a very small sketchbook if you are worried about being noticed. The chances are that you won't be, as everyone's eyes will be on the event. Nobody saw me trying to draw these ice skaters at a show, as all eyes and all the spotlights were on the fast moving skaters.

What about foreshortening?

You have to forget all the rules about standard proportions when dealing with figures at odd angles, as the shape you are seeing can be dramatically different to the standard shape that you know. Be firm and tell your brain to shut up about legs being long things if you are in front of a seated figure and all you can see of their legs is the ends of their feet!

It can help to draw a box round the figure or the foreshortened part to establish what shape you are seeing; this life model fitted into a triangular shape. Drawing the overall shape first kept me mindful of the foreshortening that I was seeing, so when my brain protested: 'But legs are long things!' I could answer: 'Not from where I'm sitting, they're not!'

Some foreshortening is extreme – in outline only it's hard to tell what this is.

Once the rest of the information is added, we have no trouble recognising these odd shapes as sunbathers.

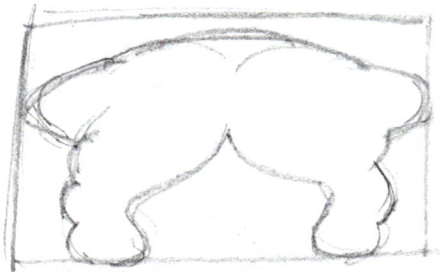

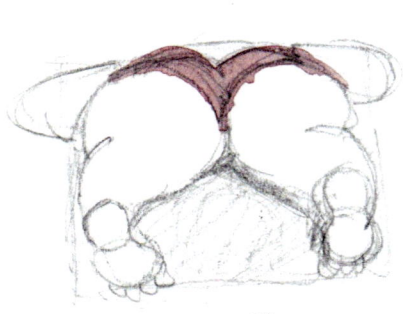

Be prepared always to question and reassess the shapes. Normal 'seeing' is a state of continual recognition and familiarity, but an artist's way of seeing is a continual state of disbelief and surprise!

Faces and heads

Drawing portraits is a specialist skill, but don't let that put you off as faces are fascinating and well worth practising. I find that drawing a face at a slight angle is easier than face on. When a head is slightly turned, there is a clear outline to guide you:

It's worth drawing a few guidelines to make sure the features end up in the right place.

Eyes are halfway down the face.

The top of the ears is level with the eyes (as every spectacle wearer knows!)

Our skull is made up of two ovals, not just one. If your figure is face on, this doesn't show, but at any other angle, if you miss out that second oval, you end up with the flat head look:

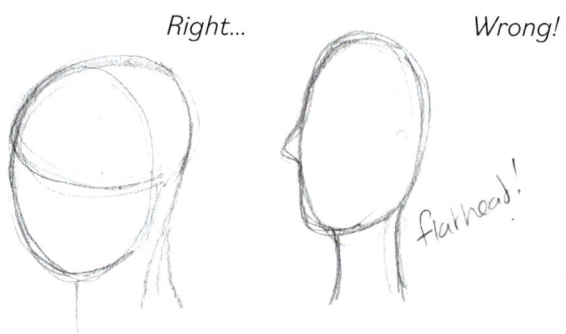

Right...   *Wrong!*

flathead!

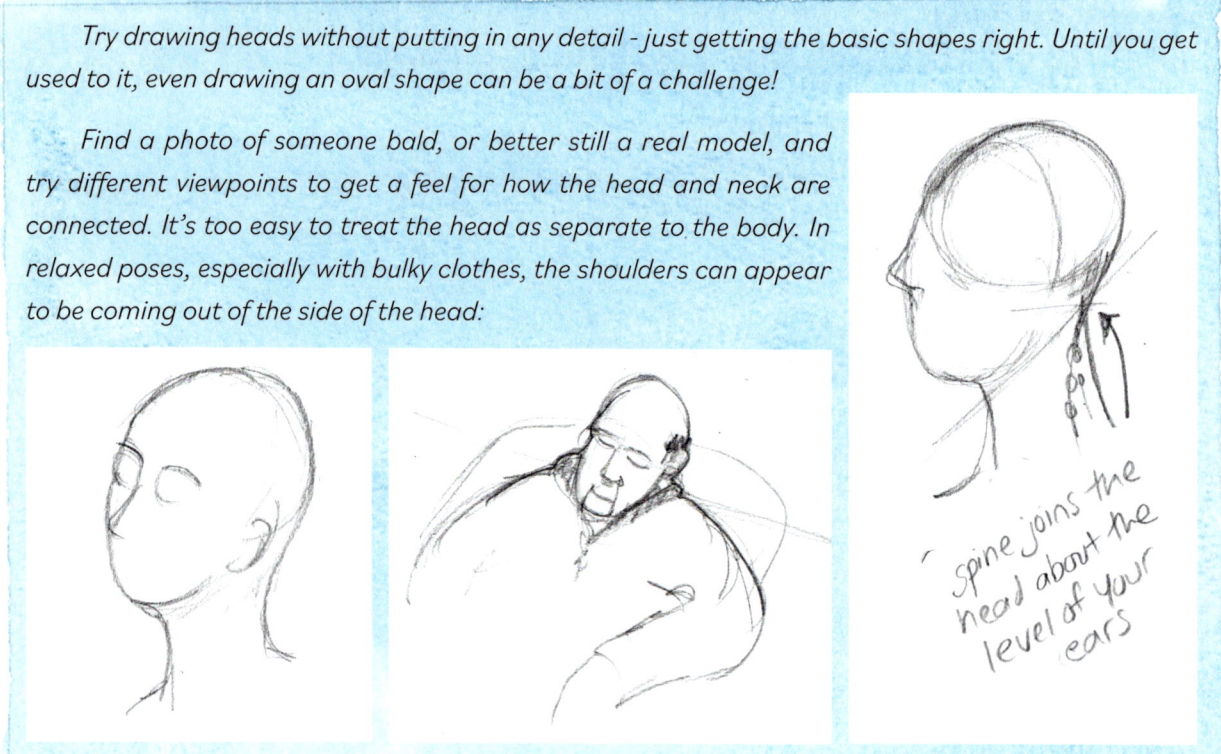

Try drawing heads without putting in any detail - just getting the basic shapes right. Until you get used to it, even drawing an oval shape can be a bit of a challenge!

Find a photo of someone bald, or better still a real model, and try different viewpoints to get a feel for how the head and neck are connected. It's too easy to treat the head as separate to the body. In relaxed poses, especially with bulky clothes, the shoulders can appear to be coming out of the side of the head:

spine joins the head about the level of your ears

Now try sketching faces in profile – every one is completely different and there is a clear 'line' to follow. Pay particular attention to the different shapes of profiles at different ages, from children to oldies, men and women. Like everything else – practice, practice, practice!

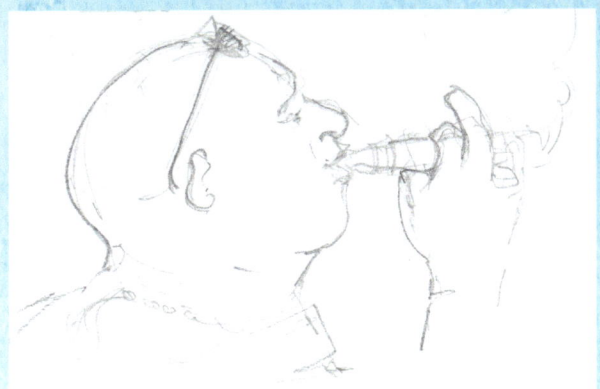

It can be fun simply to draw the profile of the face and leave the rest of the head.... There's a whole world of character in a line or two!

As you build up confidence, try drawing faces turned slightly more towards you.

Face forward

Capturing a likeness in a face takes careful study, but don't let that stop you having a go at drawing faces in portrait. Start by drawing an oval and dividing it in half to give you basic placement of eyes and nose. Look at the human face analytically and keep asking questions: how much space is there between the eyes? What shape are the eyebrows? Are there lines down the side of the mouth? How far do they go?

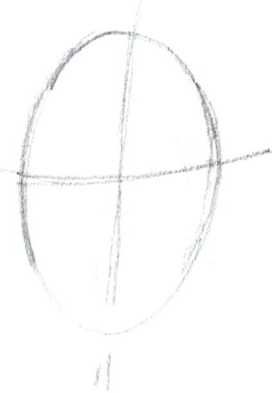

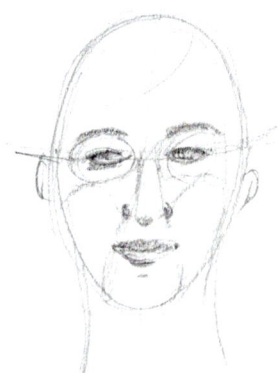

The answers to these questions will give you the basic structure of the face. Use measured drawing if you need to. In most faces you'll find that the width of the face is roughly equal to the height between chin and eyebrows, for example.

Self portraits

If you want a face to practice on, why not start with yourself? It can be embarrassing drawing a friend or family member as they will expect you to capture a likeness, and at least when drawing yourself you have a model who will sit still for as long as needed! Just place a free standing mirror on the table and have a go. Here's my attempt.

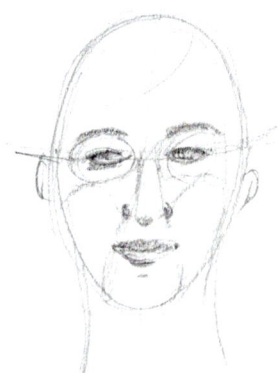

The first lines I drew were the outlines created by hair, ear and chin. I used measured drawing to check how the width of my head compared to the height. Once I was happy with the outline and basic shapes, I was able to fill in the details. When finished, I carefully rubbed out any of the early construction lines that were still showing. It's not too bad a likeness!

Figure doodling

Make a habit of doodling people wherever you're in a meeting, or waiting for someone, or at any time you need to keep your hands busy. Just do it for practice, letting your hand and pencil trace outlines, shapes and fragments.

Don't expect too much - even a poor drawing is a good drawing as it makes you take notice.

I keep a small sketchbook in my bag so that it's easy to draw without anyone noticing too much. But of course you can doodle on anything if you're caught unprepared.

The fiddle player looks as cross as if he had seen my attempt at drawing him. I was just not 'getting it' and the result is not fit to be seen. But – and it's a big BUT – it was still worth doing because every mark you make, even one you're not happy with, contributes to your experience and ability. The important thing is to keep going.

My second attempt (below) was a bit more successful at catching the musician's concentration and the angle of his hand on the bow.

Slow and careful or fast and sketchy?

Most of the time I have been urging you to take a slow and careful approach to drawing; to measure and compare, look carefully at your subject and avoid making assumptions about what you are seeing. So it may sound like a contradiction to be also telling you to go for a quick sketch, to throw yourself at a subject and be completely fearless about the result. I think you need both approaches, because all that information about measured drawing and perspective will start to become second nature and your rapid sketches will improve. You'll find yourself assessing sizes and proportions as instinctively as changing gear in a car.

Life drawing

If you get a chance, go to life-drawing sessions. Some are tutored, some are not, but if you are serious about learning to draw people you will learn much from even a few sessions. Life drawing certainly makes you look in a completely non-judgemental way at the human form and pay attention to all its complex shapes.

When I was first commissioned to illustrate a book with cartoon figures, my early characters were a bit wooden and two-dimensional. I realised that to draw good cartoon figures I needed to understand how to draw real ones so I attended life sessions and found them invaluable; my characters started to take on more life and movement.

Hands and feet

Hands and feet are a great subject to practise on as you can view them in all different positions. They are often drawn too small on figures - but they are bigger than you think. Place the bottom of your palm over your chin and you'll find you can spread your hand over most of your face.

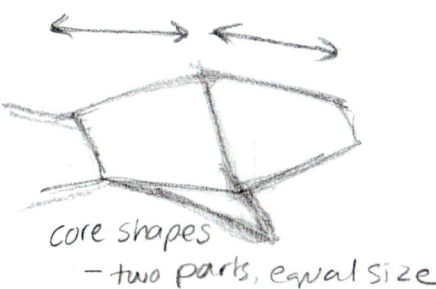

core shapes
- two parts, equal size

At it simplest, a hand is this shape:

In more detail, those shapes break down like this...

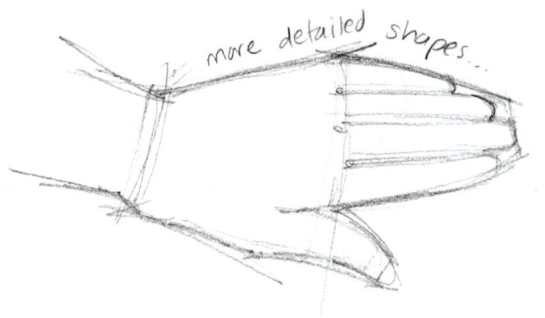

more detailed shapes...

But of course, hands move into so many different positions, you will never run short of ways to sketch them. If you struggle with the complexity, go back to asking, what is the core shape?

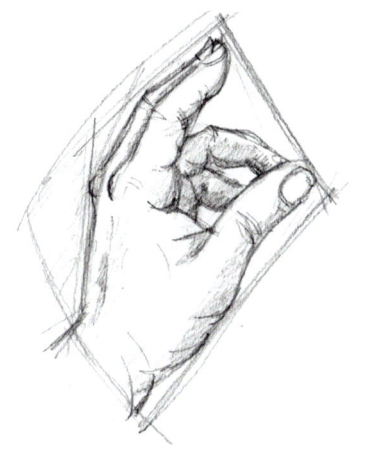

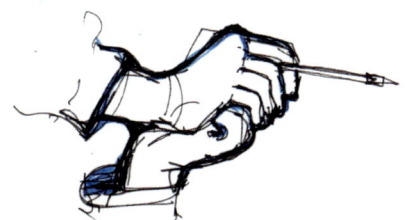

Now go back and have another go at the hand-drawing exercise in Chapter One. Find a comfortable but complex position for your hand and make a detailed drawing of it, slowly and carefully. You can look at the paper this time! But remember that you are still focussing on that connection between hand and eye and noticing every line and shape.

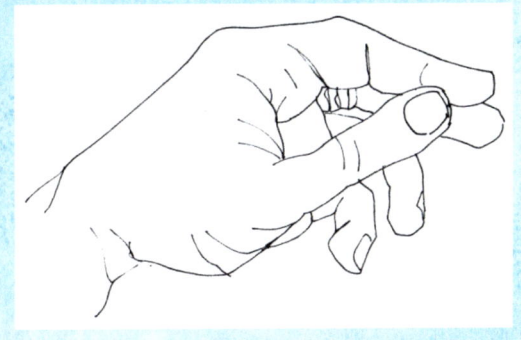

Draw your hands, other people's hands, hands holding tools or hands at rest. The possible shapes are endless!

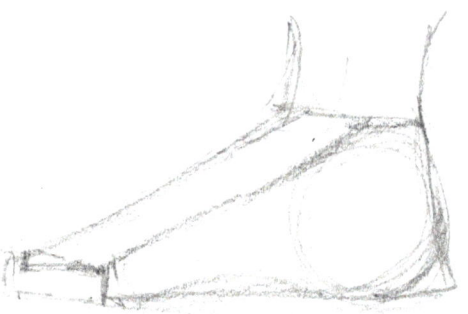

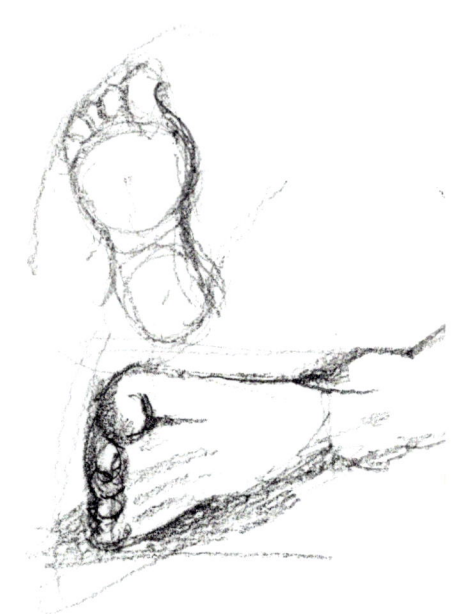

Feet are bigger than you think – did you know that they are the same size as your forearm? Sideways on they are a like a wedge of cheese... but this changes with your viewpoint.

Negative shapes

Don't forget to look for negative shapes in your figure drawing - they are as helpful here as they are anywhere else.

In this sketch I drew the two shapes between arms and head to get the position of the arms correct.

This sunbather had some tricky foreshortening of arms and legs, but those blue shapes made by the chair cushion helped to get it right.

Even the little spaces between the fingers helped with this hand drawing.

Figures in perspective

Get together with a few sketching friends or helpful family members and find a reasonably large room or open space. Position one person close to you and another (ideally about the same height) some distance back (anywhere between 5 and 20 metres is useful). Both should be facing you. The person at the front can have a guess at how much smaller the one behind is (and so far no-one has ever got this right – your brain is too tricky).

Standing in front of the two, look at what your eyes are seeing. Ignore your brain which is telling you the two are the same size. If you were to draw the pair of figures (and if they are happy to stand there for a bit longer, have a go), how far up the side of the first person would the feet of the second one start?

Even at a distance of only 10 metres or so, the second person has shrunk to about half the size of the first. Her feet will start at about the other's waist. This is the kind of information you will only notice when you are trying to draw, and it is astonishing how different it is from your 'normal' life observation.

Now before your volunteers can swap around and see this for themselves, have you noticed that the eye level of both has stayed the same? The person at the back has shrunk from the feet upwards rather than from the head down. This awareness is helpful when placing figures in a scene.

This is only a very brief introduction to figure drawing, of course, but I hope there are enough techniques here to get you started and overcome the fear of what is perceived to be a difficult subject. If you want to find out more, there are plenty of specialist books on the subject and I recommend life-drawing or figure-drawing classes - they are not as daunting as they seem!

WILDLIFE PARK IN CRUISE TERMINAL, CARTAGENA

Flamingos, parrots

peacocks, monkeys...

CWM-YR-EGLWYS
Dinas Head, Pembrokeshire

weather-worn Bible on firedeck!

model ship at Cwm yr Eglwys

Chapter Six: Beyond Pencils

There has never been so much choice of art materials. Pencils are cheap, accessible and perfect for all kinds of drawing, but it's good to broaden your skills, add colour and find new ways to make marks on paper. Art shops and stationery suppliers are stuffed with a confusing choice of materials, so here's a guide to different types and recommendations for the ones that I've found most useful. Try as many as you can – if you like the feel of the materials you're using, you'll spend more time with them and they'll become, as all tools should, an extension of your hand.

Sketchbooks and paper

Most sketchbooks contain smooth, white, cartridge paper, designed to take pencils, pens, coloured pencils and a certain amount of wet media like watercolour. The quality of the paper varies greatly, which might not matter while you're in the early stages of practising, but as you gain confidence and want to keep your sketchbooks then it's worth buying good quality books. It's disappointing when a sketchbook binding falls apart, or you find it contains thin, poor quality paper.

Some sketchbooks contain specialist paper for pastels, acrylics, or watercolour, which are great for their intended purpose but their texture can make them unsuitable for pencil drawing – pencils love smooth white paper, not too thin, not too shiny. Or for something different, try tinted paper.

I recommend buying hardback sketchbooks rather than spiral bound or loose leaf. Firstly, it gives you the option of spreading a drawing across two pages if you want to work big or capture a panoramic scene.

Secondly, it's tempting with spiral bound to tear out the pages you're not happy with and you end up with a thin empty book. I know – I've done it!

If you want to make a finished drawing to frame or give to someone, of course, you'll need a good quality loose-leaf pad or sheets of paper (try Bristol board which is a heavy weight, very white paper designed for crisp pencil or pen work). If you like working on loose sheets of paper, attach them to a lightweight drawing board with tape or bulldog clips. Or use a clipboard, available in A4 or A3 size.

paper & clipboard
(A4 or A3)

Or draw on anything at all – pages from old books, travel tickets, brown paper, napkins, hand made paper, the back of an envelope, a shopping list... However you do it, if you have access to paper and pencil, you'll never be bored again! (If you do work on loose scraps of paper, then you can paste them into a sketchbook, scrap book style).

*A cross-channel ferry ticket gave me a
surprising source of sketching inspiration!*

What about sketchbook size? You can buy every size from tiny pocket books to A3, in shapes from landscape to portrait to square or panoramic. Try different ones and see what suits – you'll probably find you need several. I carry a small one in my handbag, a larger one for general sketching and travel diaries, and then an A3 in the studio for design roughs and book layouts.

This is a selection of my small sketchbooks, both well known brands and hand made – I can't resist buying them and keep them all to use 'one day'.

If you love paper and bookbinding, you can make your own sketchbooks. Concertina books are easy to make and fun to use.

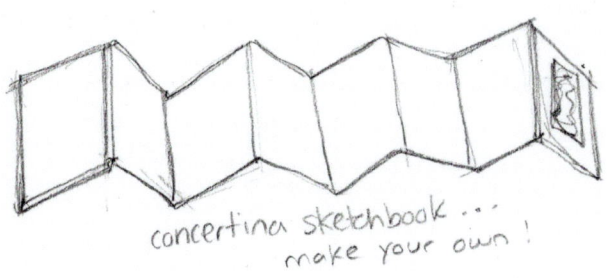

Sketching pens

You can draw with any kind of pen – biro, felt tip, gel pens, fountain pens – but sketching pens are particularly versatile and easy to use. They come in a range of point sizes from 0.05 (very thin) to 1.0 (fat). They're cheap to buy and last quite well.

I find nib size 0.2 most useful for sketching, but you can buy sets with a range of nib sizes so you can experiment with what suits your style.

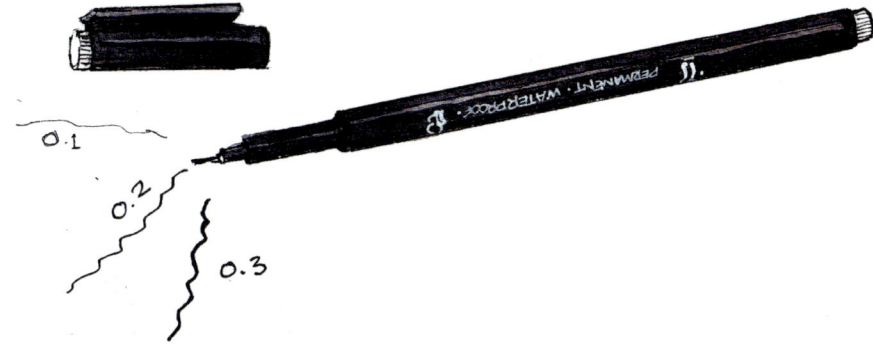

As well as black pens, you can also buy sepia, grey and full colour sets.

Waterproof or non waterproof?

Some pens will have 'permanent' or 'waterproof' on them, some won't. If they don't, assume that they will smudge when wet. It's useful to know this if you are planning to add watercolour - you may want the pen lines to smudge and soften, but if you don't, then make sure you use waterproof pens.

I add watercolours to my pen sketches sometimes, so I need waterproof pens to get this effect:

You can add colour to pen drawings, or add lines to colour sketches - try both. Sometimes a few pen lines can be very effective. But don't draw into a wet surface or you'll damage the nib.

Before the invention of felt-tipped pens, ink drawing needed nibs and ink. These are still available and if you get the opportunity, try a dip pen with a drawing nib and Indian ink. The springiness of the nib gives a variety of line thickness that is very expressive, and you also have the option of diluting the ink with a brush to add tone. Experiment with this as well as fountain pens and various makes of brush pen if you think it might suit your style, though I don't recommend trying to work with dip pens and pots of ink on location!

Unlike pencils which can produce shades of light and dark, pens only do black, so to get the impression of tone you'll need to be a bit creative. Using a selection of sketching pens, draw five small boxes, just like you did for the tonal exercise in chapter 4. Shade in the darkest square and leave the lightest one white.

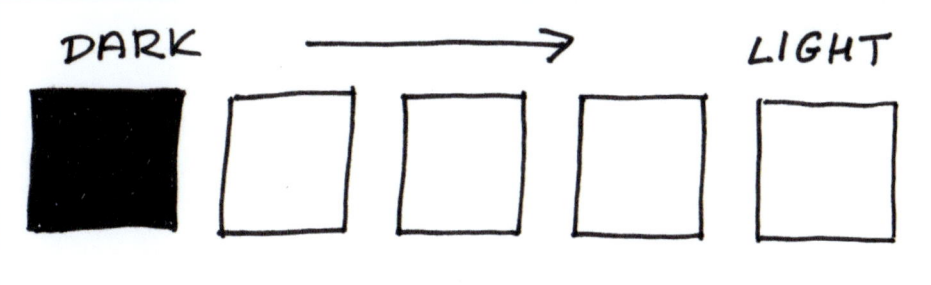

That bit was easy, but how are you going to fill in the shades of grey from dark to light?

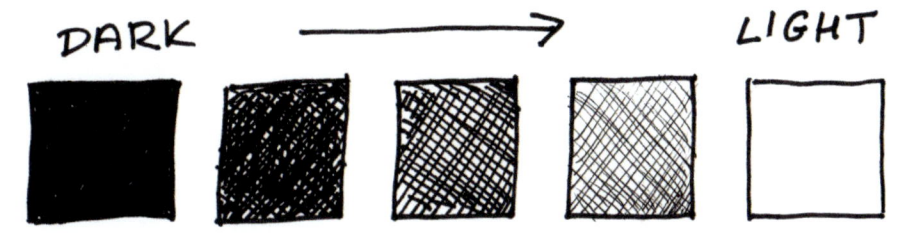

One way is by cross-hatching – I used a 0.5 nib and heavier lines for the darker squares, then a 0.2 nib and more space between the lines for the lightest shade. Try it, see how many ways you can achieve tonal variation with a black line.

The kind of tonal marks you make need to show the nature of the object you're drawing where possible – for example, standard cross hatching doesn't look too good on a tree....

But a more rounded scribbly line is more expressive.

Stippling – shading with lots of tiny dots – requires a great deal of time and patience but it's very effective, especially for soft-edged clouds and light.

Cross hatching works well on these cliffs.

Different ways with pens

1. The direct approach

Take a deep breath and start to draw. You can't rub out, you can't do faint lines, you just have to go for it. If you make a mistake, ignore it and carry on. If you're prone to rubbing out your pencil lines too much, you'll find this way of drawing surprisingly liberating – especially if you don't worry about the results! It helps if you remember to draw nearer objects first.

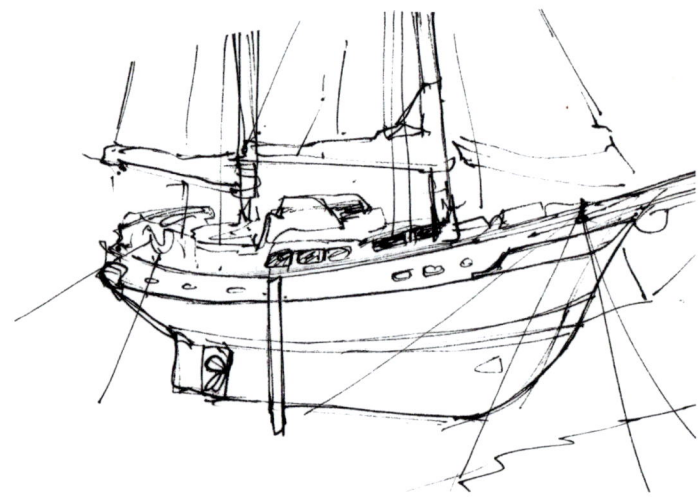

Then try rapid line sketches of moving objects or people.

2. The careful approach

For more accurate line drawings, I work in pencil first, very lightly, then go over with the pens.

I've used a mix of pencil and pen in this sketch of moving boats – drawing them lightly with pencil first and then later, back on shore, adding pen lines whilst the shapes were still fresh in my memory.

For more finished illustration work I draw lightly in pencil first, then add more careful pen lines and, as a final step, rub out all the pencil lines.

When drawing buildings, it can help to draw the structural lines lightly in pencil first – use a ruler if you need to. Then you can draw freehand with the pen using the pencil lines as a guide.

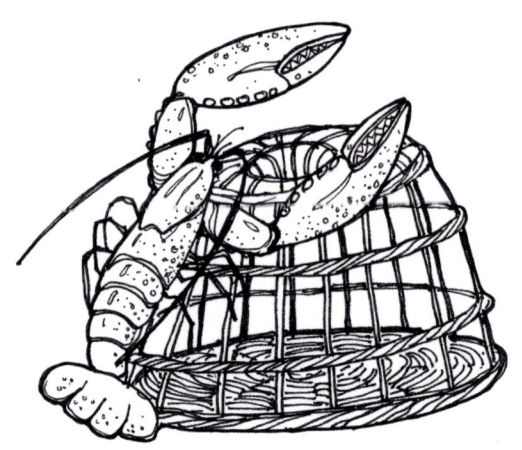

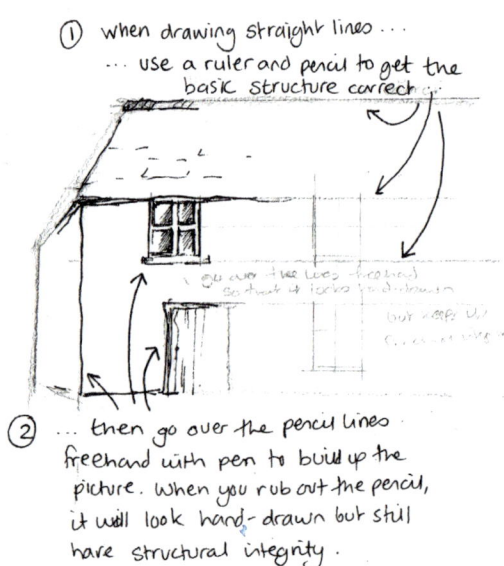

You can of course use the ruler for the pen lines too (I do this when drawing the mast of a boat), but it can look more natural, particularly on an old building, to keep the pen lines freehand, just using the pencil as a guide.

Drawing with colour

Drawing doesn't have to be in black and white, and colour is not something that's only for finished paintings. Colour adds life to a sketchbook, so I encourage you to experiment with different ways of using colour to develop your own style and way of working. A brush can be a very expressive drawing tool - try it with inks, watercolours, any liquid medium (but if using indian ink or acrylic ink, be sure to wash the brushes well after use).

These cats were 'drawn' direct in watercolour and brush, with a few pen marks added later when it was dry.

Watercolours

I won't go into too much detail here about using watercolours – yes, it's true that they can be tricky to use, but on the other hand if you think less about 'painting' and more about simply drawing with colour, or adding a few spots of colour to a line drawing, it all becomes more manageable.

Start with a small paintbox and a couple of brushes. A Windsor and Newton Cotman watercolour set is an affordable way to get used to watercolours, as the quality is good for a beginner set. Use enough water with the paint to let the colours flow without feeling scratchy or covering up the lines you've drawn.

A paintbox will come with its own colours, some of which you'll never use. You can replace these with your own choices as you become more familiar with them. You'll gradually create your own palette but these are the colours I use, which give me just about every colour I ever need:

- Reds: alizarin crimson, cadmium red, burnt sienna
- Blues: ultramarine, cerulean, cobalt, indigo and windsor blue-green shade
- Yellows: aureolin, cadmium yellow, raw sienna

You don't usually use white in watercolours as you leave the white of the paper, diluting the colours to get paler shades. I carry a white marker pen in my drawing kit for making white marks on dark colours.

Watercolours work particularly well with waterproof sketching pens – have a go. Usually you would draw first, then add colour afterwards – but you can do it the other way round. Try everything!

You don't have to colour everything in a drawing – just highlight whatever grabbed your attention. On a dull February day, the bright orange buoy caught my eye and made me notice the complex shapes of the landing stage. I didn't feel the need to add any more colour.

Coloured pencils

Coloured pencils go far beyond the 'colouring in' role that we learned at school. Buy them from an art shop rather than using a children's set as the quality will be so much better and you'll get more depth of colour.

Water-soluble coloured pencils are particularly useful, especially when you're short of time or don't have space to get paints out. Getting a few colours down on paper will be more effective than trying to draw the scene in black and white. The added advantage of watercolour pencils is that you can add water with a brush later and blend the colours around.

Choose a simple object, or collection of objects, to draw. A jug, a bowl of fruit, something with simple shapes. Don't use a pencil, but draw straight in with water soluble coloured pencils. It doesn't matter which colour! I use Derwent Inktense which are very vibrant colours, but there are lots of different makes available. Some cheaper ones may be a little pale, though.

Once you have the shapes, add a few touches of colour and with a wet brush soften the marks you've made.

When the colours are dry, add more marks, which you can leave dry or wet again if you want to. Try drawing the same object with different colour backgrounds, or imagining new backgrounds. Do one where you only add colour to the background and negative shapes (spaces inbetween) and leave

the object white. Play around with the textures you get by wetting the colours only partially so that the marks still show. Enjoy yourself! Don't worry about being too realistic, let your creativity off the leash.

I did several drawings of this jug, both on its own and with other objects, to give an interesting variety of shapes. I had fun playing around with different colours for each version.

This was done with Derwent 'Inktense' watercolour pencils, used on location with a bit of water blended in later - I wanted to keep some of the sketchy marks so I didn't use too much water.

Magic pencils

I recently discovered the fun you can have with Koh-I-Nor magic pencils – these are probably meant for children but they're great for drawing in colour. They have multi-coloured 'leads' so that the colour changes as you draw. There are many shades to choose from but the two pictured here are my favourites.

Sometimes they give you the colours you want, but most of the time, although the pencils don't give you the 'right' colours, they can liven up a sketch and, like all the materials I've mentioned in this chapter, help you bridge the gap between 'drawing' and 'painting'.

Experiment

There are many more art materials to try than I've listed here, as I've only shown you the ones I use regularly. There are felt-tip pens, pastels, oil pastels, inks - try out as many as you can and see what works for you.

First onion from Frances' garden ...... and it's going inh the tortilla

upstairs at Museum

turkey vulture

feather

CHAPTER SEVEN: DIFFERENT WAYS OF DRAWING

Drawing in public

One of the reasons why beginners are reluctant to draw outside is the fear of exposure. For some reason artists are seen as public property and a curious passer-by will sooner or later peer over your shoulder and say 'mind if I have a look?' (and it's too late by then to say 'yes, I do mind, actually.')

You find yourself apologising, embarrassed ('oh it's rubbish really, I'm just a beginner, I can't draw at all, ha ha...') and you decide that from now on you're going to photograph the scene and work only at the privacy of your kitchen table.

Stick with it – there are ways to overcome the fear:

- Find a place to draw where you're tucked away with your back to the wall, or somewhere remote where no-one can easily peer over your shoulder

- Gain confidence in private spaces like a friend's garden or home.

- Get together with a group of like-minded friends and go sketching together.

- Interiors have plenty of subject matter. Choose a quiet day for a visit to a museum or historic building, arrange a private visit to a local church or landmark.

Museums have subjects to sketch that you'd never find anywhere else.

- Treat your sketchbook as a diary and write as much as you draw. Sketching is seen as public, but the minute you start writing, people see that as private and will back off.

- Keep your sketching gear simple. A small sketchbook and pencil will be far less conspicuous than an easel, canvas and palette. If you want to complete a painting on location, obviously you'll need more gear, but to begin with keep it simple, keep it small.

Try drawing somewhere outside your home, just for five minutes. Stop at the end of five minutes. Do it again the next day for ten minutes. Build up the time you sketch on each occasion so that you start to feel a little more confident. After all, five minutes is enough to get a few lines on paper, but not long enough to attract attention. If someone does approach, stop drawing and start writing.

Five minutes is enough time for a sketch!

Drawing from photos

Photos are a huge asset to artists. They are invaluable as a source of reference material. How great artists of the past would have loved them! (I recommend David Hockney's book *Secret Knowledge* which looks at how the great masters used lenses to project their images onto canvas and trace over them). Cameras capture subjects in motion, remember detail that we didn't have time to draw, enable us to draw subjects we love whilst stuck indoors.

A lovely scene, dull photo, good sketch!

Treat your camera as an information provider. Yes, you will of course get a more accurate drawing by copying from a photo, but if you get out there and try it from life as well, your drawings will be the better for it. We see life differently from the way a camera sees it, and a sketch reflects this. Taking a photo to paint from 'later' can make you lazy - after all, a photo is already in 2D. This saves you the trouble of having to analyse what you see, noticing shapes and relationships, discovering a new way of looking at the familiar – the part of being an artist that's hard work, exciting, frustrating and satisfying all at the same time. Even if a small part of your drawing practice is done on location, it will add life to your work.

Don't be a slave to the photo - feel free to crop, edit, change the composition.

Find a photo that you took to use as drawing reference, but don't draw it exactly as it is. Take out things you don't want (the parked car, the boat on the shore) and add others (distant figures, birds, more trees). Imagination is as much a part of drawing as observation.

Here I just used the basic shape of the two boats that caught my eye, and simplified what I could 'see' in the space between them.

Now let's try it the other way round - drawing first, photo second. Choose a subject and draw it from life. Then take a photo and print it out to about the same size as your drawing and compare the two, see how you did. As I've said before, you don't need to be as accurate as a camera, but if you are repeatedly coming unstuck with proportions or perspective, this can help you to work out where you keep going wrong.

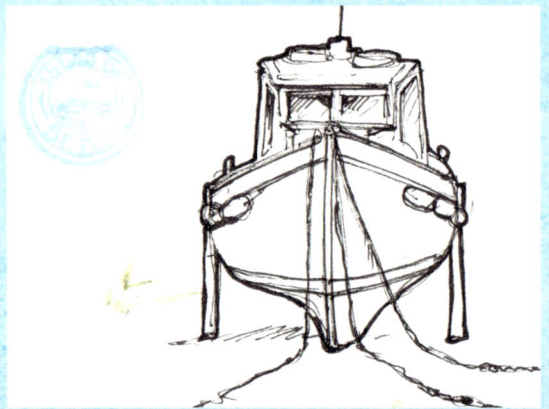

Here's my attempt. I can see from the photo that I've not made the boat wide enough and the shape of the bow is too steep. I obviously wasn't concentrating! It was a pleasant, if breezy, afternoon on a lovely beach in the Isles of Scilly.

Next time you go somewhere new, have a photo-free day. If you see something interesting, have a go at sketching it, or simply look at it, slowly and deliberately. We think we take photos to remember things better, but sometimes you'll remember more by spending time with or without your sketch book.

Drawing a theme

Sketching anything, everywhere is marvellous for practice, but it can also be fun to keep a separate sketchbook for a particular subject or idea, or choose a theme to follow for a week or a month.

Here are a few suggestions:

- your garden (through the seasons, stages of growth, close up studies of plants or seeds)
- food (ingredients, what's on the chopping board, fruit, veg, meals, kitchen scenes)
- beachcombing (pebbles, shells, feathers, driftwood, rubbish)
- windows and doors (houses, cottages, churches, old buildings, archways)
- boots and shoes
- favourite walks - choose a different subject to focus on each time
- jugs, teaspoons, collections of objects
- patterns and fabrics, rugs and scarves
- birds, animals, pets

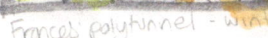

Every walk becomes a quest.... I love discovering archways!

You'll never take a familiar walk for granted if you go hunting for a different subject every time. Stay on the lookout for your chosen subject and collect reference material wherever you go.

Drawing from the imagination

This is something we found easy to do as a child but might find more challenging now. Drawing doesn't have to represent 'real' things; if you have a desire to draw imaginary characters, tell a story, create mermaids and dragons, fantasy worlds, or express thoughts and ideas, then do it! Doodling helps – take a line for a walk and see where it goes.

Next time you are watching TV, on the phone, or listening to music, give your hand a pen and paper and let it doodle without you worrying what comes out. Pens work well for this exercise as they give you nice clear lines, and coloured pencils are great too. If you struggle to get going with random doodles, find inspiration in household objects, patterns on fabrics, shapes, natural objects like leaves or flowers, photos or words. Doodling is a great stressbuster as well as helping you to become fluent in your style of drawing.

I should have been paying attention to a meeting, not thinking about fish and boat shapes when I doodled in my notebook. I make no apology for being a bad influence, but doodling in a meeting may not be a good idea if you're in the chair!'

Drawing words and poetry

If you want to take imaginative drawing further, just add more words – poems work well but so do quotations, songs and stories. When you read words, images form in the theatre of your mind and the challenge can be to express these on paper, as an illustrator would.

Take a poem, quotation or piece of prose you like, spend some time seeing what images the words summon in your mind. Then play around with putting those images on paper. Don't judge what comes out, treat it as creative play.

ToRosario

early in the morning · the moon was in the sky

and all I ask is a tall ship

and a star to steer her by

Journeys, maps and stories

I love making illustrated maps in my sketchbook of any journey I make. This is one of the reasons I always carry a sheet of tracing paper with my sketching gear so that I can trace the outlines that I need from an atlas, website or guide book – I don't worry about detail, just the basic shapes. I can then transfer the lines to my page and embellish them as much as I want to. Great for memories!

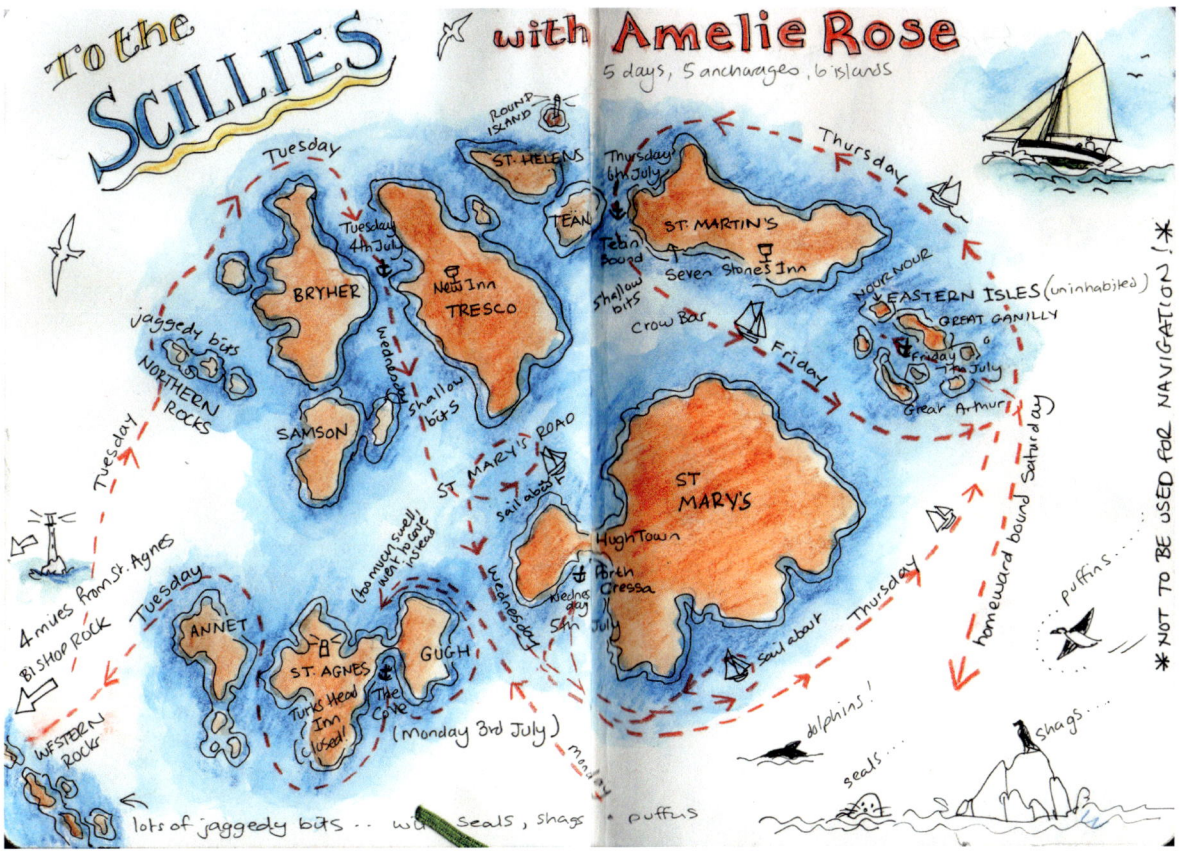

Create a map of your favourite place – even it's your garden, your favourite local walk, a place you go on holiday. Add words, colour, little drawings, doodles, cartoons, anything that belongs with the location. Don't worry too much about how it looks, enjoy the visual journey!

If you don't want to draw the map, tear up a real map and paste that in your sketchbook, draw on top of it or around it. There's no right or wrong way, only your way of making your world visible.

Egrets, I've had a few…….

'It's a simple and generous rule of life that whatever you practice, you will improve at.'

(Elizabeth Gilbert)

Never give up… this sketch is one of my early attempts. Well, at least you can see what it's meant to be!

CHAPTER EIGHT: CELEBRATE YOUR MISTAKES

'I am always doing that which I cannot do, in order that I may learn how to do it.'

(Picasso)

The thrill of learning a new skill – especially when we learn as adults – is often sabotaged by an over-fierce inner critic. We want to be good at something quickly, and when we're not, because life doesn't work like that, there's a little voice in our head which tempts us to give up.

In order to enjoy your drawing journey as fully as possible, you need to change your attitude to 'failure'.

The only way to improve your drawing skills is to learn to accept your mistakes, cheerfully and wholeheartedly. It's only paper! Turn the page and try again. Get all those wrong drawings out of the way so that you can get to the better ones that lie underneath. If you feel despondent and inhibited by your first attempts (they're wonky, child-like, tentative, just hopeless…) then you'll give up and the imp in your head, which said you couldn't do it, will say 'I told you so!'

Upgrade your inner critic

We all have one, we all need one. If you didn't know that your drawing looked nothing like the object you were trying to draw, you'd never improve. BUT most people have an inner critic like a chattering monkey, knocking you down every time you try and grow something new. He

howler monkeys at Cahuita

spoils your life, but the more you fight him, the louder he jabbers.

Here's what you need to do – replace him with a wiser, kinder mentor. Your inner critic should be your most useful ally, not your enemy.

Mine is a kind of quiet, reflective Yoda-like character who raises a questioning eyebrow at me if I'm tempted to push on with a commission when I know there's a major error in proportion somewhere. He (or occasionally she) doesn't put me down, ever, just reminds me kindly to check, make corrections, not take myself or my work too seriously. He gives a nudge if I lose concentration. He gives me the courage and humility to throw something in the bin even if I've spent all day on it, take out another piece of paper and try again.

Be curious

You don't mind this more kindly mentor peering over your shoulder when you draw. Instead of personal remarks and put-downs, he (or she) will offer a different quality of criticism, in the way of kindly curiosity. Like this: 'Hmm, that doesn't look quite right... let's take another look. The wrong shape there, perhaps, and that bit is too big compared to that bit. Let's measure more carefully this time and try again. Not bad for a first go!'

Learning is a process of repetition with curiosity. Repetition and practice alone won't get you very far if you keep on making the same mistakes every time. When looking at your work, listen only to the wise, non-judgemental voice which replaces criticism with curiosity, congratulates you on having done it in the first place and wonders with interest what you can do to correct any technical errors. Curiosity will encourage you to have another go, this

time with more awareness of the things you weren't paying attention to. Curiosity is endlessly patient and interested in the process of connecting hand an eye; it will keep you at it, carefully and mindfully, long after the criticising imp has gone off in a huff.

Apply this inquisitiveness to art and creativity of all kinds. Go to exhibitions and workshops, look at sketchbook work by current and past artists if you can. Find out what excites you or inspires you and try to work out why.

Draw like you mean it

Having spent many chapters showing you how to get your drawing accurate, it may sound strange to be now saying it's not the most important thing. Working on technical accuracy gives you a solid foundation, helps you to develop as an artist, and establishes the habit of observation, but it's easy to get obsessed by how 'good' or 'bad' your drawings are. Don't forget to draw like you mean it, for the sheer pleasure of making marks on paper. Drawing has the potential to be so much more than just a two-dimensional copy of a three-dimensional object.

Painted on a scrap of wood, and not meant to be a realistic painting of a ship, a little picture by Alfred Wallis stood out for me amongst all the exhibits in the room. I stopped to sketch it, tried to understand why it had so much life and 'truth' in it, and why I liked it so much.

We all have 'bad pencil days'

There will be times when your drawings just don't seem to flow, when whatever you do turns out wrong. It happens to me too – sometimes I push on through, sometimes I turn my attention to something else instead. If you get a page that just doesn't work, accept it – some days are a struggle, some are a joy. Your sketchbook will be reflecting your life, that's all.

My favourite Picasso quote! (playing around with a possible apron design)

Beware of 'waiting for inspiration'. It's too easy to say 'I'll wait until I feel in the mood for drawing.' The chances are that you won't feel in the mood. So sometimes, just do it anyway. Because the longer you leave it, the harder it gets.

Slow down and pay attention

Drawing requires concentration. There's a part of you that loves to draw, finds it exciting and satisfying; it's like throwing open the windows and letting in light and air to a room in your mind that used to be dark and closed up. But there's also the lazy, impatient part of your brain that can't be bothered and will trick you into rushing it, putting any old thing down on the page. Don't fall for it!

One of my students drew a Thames barge, a local traditional sailing boat that used to carry cargo on the east coast. They're sturdy and handsome craft with a very distinctive shape. 'I'm not happy with it', she said, 'but I'm not sure why. Boats are difficult!'

'What shape is the bow - the front of the boat?' I asked. She glanced at her photograph. 'It's straight up and down'. 'So why have you drawn yours curved?' 'Oh, I didn't notice that!' she said. Exactly! It was a lazy brain getting in the way. 'Oh, it's just a boat, this is a boat shape, it'll do'. Once we straightened out the curved bow, the drawing worked. Some details wouldn't have been so important - but this was one of the main features of the boat.

So the good news is that the problem is easily sorted when it finally hits home that you have to notice things – and given a little effort, we can all do that. No talent needed!

Avoid lazy-brain syndrome by continually asking questions when you're drawing: 'What shape is that? Where does this line join that one? What's that little shape inbetween? How tall is that in relation to that?' Compare, compare, compare.

There's no such word as 'should'

You may only want to sketch when you go on holiday; I know plenty of people who do. If you're one of them, that's fine, don't feel guilty about not doing it the rest of the time. You will still find the exercises in this book useful if you choose to do them and you will still take pleasure in what you do. But if you are someone who would really like to do more, feel that you 'should' be sketching far more frequently but somehow life gets in the way and there's never the time, don't beat yourself up. There are ways you can wedge a bit more drawing into you day. Guilt and regret never made anyone into a good artist. Say 'I want to do more sketching' instead of 'I should do more sketching'. The words 'want to' have a lot more energy attached to them!

- *Leave sketching materials ready and open around the home so that you can draw in the inbetween times, when dinner is cooking or there are a few spare minutes before the next thing you have to do. If your art materials live in a cupboard and life is busy, they tend to stay there. Then you feel guilty every time you look at the cupboard and that just makes it even harder.*

- *Keep a small sketchbook in your bag or pocket so that you can draw whilst you're waiting for someone, in a cafe or in the car, at a concert, anywhere anytime. Just a few minutes will do.*

- *Decide that you are going to draw for fifteen minutes a day for a set period – say, a week. After all, fifteen minutes is nothing; it goes in a flash, and is a manageable amount of time to steal from the day. You'll probably surprise yourself and find that half an hour has passed before you know it.*

- *Don't worry about not having time to finish a drawing. Half-finished is fine, so is just a few lines on the page! At least you've begun.*

- *Don't spend hours looking for the perfect subject - sometimes you can find it right in front of you.*

Buttons and beads

Drawing makes you happy

Remember that drawing is not a competitive sport. You are drawing because you want to appreciate and connect to your surroundings. You are drawing to spend time with something you enjoy, where nothing else matters and all life's cares will stop their chatter for just a while. Enjoy the journey, fill your sketchbooks, take up the challenge of noticing the world with your hands and eyes, and you will never be bored again.

THE SPIRIT OF DISCOVERY

I t's not easy to keep the learning going when you're on your own - life tends to get in the way. I've listed here a few suggestions for books, websites and ways to make your creative journey easier to travel.

Art holidays

Going on sketching holidays with like-minded people is a great way to stay inspired. I work regularly with Art Safari (**artsafari.co.uk**) who run excellent tutored art holidays all over the world, as well as workshops at their studio in Suffolk.

viv sketching in the rain.

Books

- **Keeping a Sketchbook Diary**, Claudia Myatt (Golden Duck)
- **A Short Book About Drawing**, Andrew Marr (Quadrille)
- **Elements of Drawing**, John Ruskin (notes by Bernard Dunstan) (Herbert)
- **Drawing on the Right Side of the Brain**, Betty Edwards (Fontana)
- **Drawing People**, Lynne Chapman (Search Press)
- **Big Magic: Creative Living Beyond Fear**, Elizabeth Gilbert (Bloomsbury)
- **Secret Knowledge: Rediscovering the lost techniques of the Old Masters**, David Hockney (Thames & Hudson)

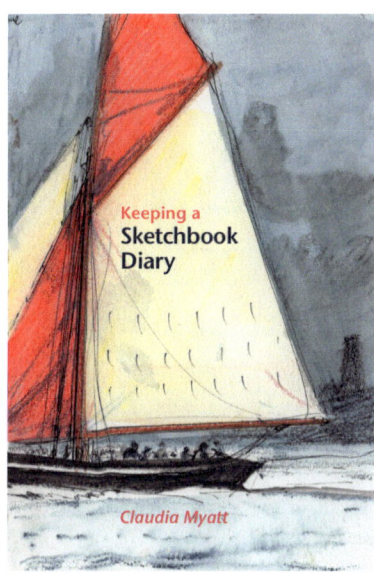

Keeping a Sketchbook Diary

Claudia Myatt

Websites

There are so many websites, tutorials and events about drawing and art online that I've just picked a few that I've found most useful.

Of course I'm bound to recommend my own website **claudiamyatt.co.uk**. I keep a regular blog and the 'tuition' page lists all my classes, workshops and art holidays. I also have a **youtube** channel with various short tutorials in watercolours and sketching. Just search on 'Claudia Myatt' in **youtube.com** and you'll find them.

The Campaign for Drawing was launched in 2000 to commemorate the work of John Ruskin and promote his belief that drawings helps us to understand and see the world more clearly. It runs 'The Big Draw' event every year to 'raise the profile of drawing as a tool for thought, creativity, social and cultural engagement'. **thebigdraw.org**

Urban Sketchers is a worldwide organisation which encourages people to get together and sketch on location. **urbansketchers.org**. The main website is based in the USA but there is plenty going on in the UK – have a look at **lynnechapmanurbansketching.co.uk**.

London based **royaldrawingschool.org** offers a good range of drawing and art courses both online and in person.

Social media

Facebook can be a good place to find others locally who might like to meet up for sketching and mutual support. I belong to a local group called Suffolk Sketchers who get together at a different venue each month and also share images online. If you don't have a group already, then start one!

I'm on facebook as Claudia Myatt Illustration and also run a page called **'Learn to sketch with Claudia Myatt'** which has regular tips.

Acknowledgements

I started this book a few years before publication as I found there was an increasing demand for drawing workshops and my students wanted to have reference material to help them continue their learning. But because I was so busy teaching, there was never time to finish the book – until the Covid-19 pandemic early in 2020 put everything on hold and suddenly I had time to Get On With It. So thank you Julia Jones of Golden Duck Publishing for taking it on and helping me to get it into print, especially as everything always takes longer than you think!

Thanks to Mary-Anne Bartlett of Art Safari, herself a superb artist and teacher, who has filled my diary with workshops, sent me off to teach art holidays and found plenty of keen students for me to try out all my techniques on. Thanks too for our many wine-fuelled sketching schemes!

To all the artists, teachers and students over the years who have crossed my path and added to my knowledge, I am truly grateful.

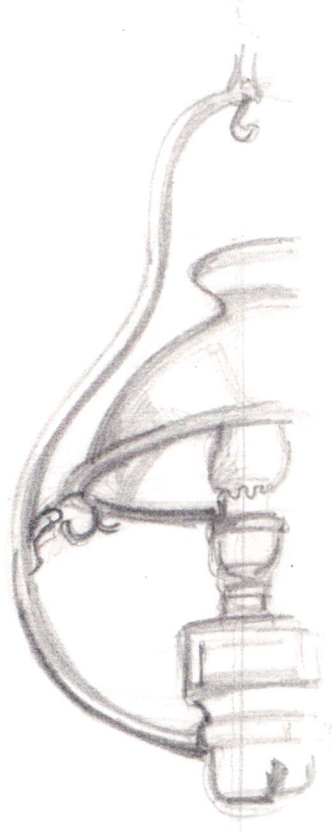

- Remind yourself often that a drawing doesn't have to be technically perfect to be worth doing.

- Carry a sketchbook with you wherever you go - and use it! Don't be daunted by those empty white pages. It's only paper!

- Doodle, play with shapes, tones, colours. Spend as much time as possible with your drawing tools until they become an extension of your hand.

- Talk to other artists, ask questions, watch people draw, stay curious.

- Draw from life as much as possible.

- Notice things. Don't make assumptions about what you are seeing. Look properly, question everything.

- Compare width and height of any two lines or shapes to help get basic proportions right.

- Flatten your world and switch off your 3D vision. See everything as interconnected shapes, even the spaces in between.

- Drawing is like any other language or manual skill - fluency comes with practice. Keep at it!

- Above all, enjoy the act of drawing - it's something that humans have been doing since the beginning of time and probably always will.

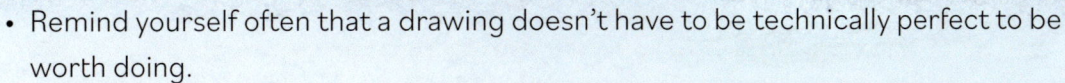

Claudia

Also published by Golden Duck

The Strong Winds Series: (adventure fiction for older children or adults)

written by Julia Jones, illustrated by Claudia Myatt

- *The Salt-Stained Book* (also available in audio) £8.99
- *A Ravelled Flag* £8.99
- *Ghosting Home* £7.99
- *The Lion of Sole Bay* £7.99
- *Black Waters* £8.99
- *Pebble* £8.99

The Allingham Biography series: (general non-fiction)

- *The Adventures of Margery Allingham*
  by Julia Jones (foreword by Nicci Gerrard) £14.99
- *Cheapjack*
  by Philip Allingham (introduction by Francis Wheen) £12.99
- *The Oaken Heart*
  by Margery Allingham (foreword by Ronald Blythe) £14.99
- *Fifty Years in the Fiction Factory*
  by Julia Jones (foreword by Professor Jenny Hartley) £17.99
- *Beloved Old Age – and What to Do About It*
  by Julia Jones & Margery Allingham £9.99

Other fiction and non-fiction:

- *Wild Wood* (an alternative view of *The Wind in the Willows*)
  written by Jan Needle, illustrated by Willie Rushton £9.99
- *Keeping a Sketchbook Diary*
  by Claudia Myatt £9.99
- *The Cruise of Naromis: August in the Baltic 1939*
  by G.A. Jones (introduction & afterword by Julia Jones) £9.99
- *Please Tell Me & Please Tell Me More*
  (two activity books / scrapbooks for older people) £3.99
- *Waldringfield: a Suffolk Village by the River Deben*
  by the Waldringfield History Group (forthcoming 29/9/2020)

Most titles also available in e-format. Visit www.golden-duck.co.uk for more information or contact Julia Jones, Sokens, Green Street, Pleshey, nr Chelmsford, Essex CM3 1HT. 01245-231898